W9-CFU-506

CLIO'S CONSORT

JEREMY BELKNAP, by Henry Sargent, 1798.
Collection of the Massachusetts Historical Society.

CLIO'S CONSORT:

JEREMY BELKNAP

AND THE FOUNDING OF

THE MASSACHUSETTS HISTORICAL

SOCIETY

by

Louis Leonard Tucker

BOSTON, MASSACHUSETTS

Published by the Society

1990

Distributed by Northeastern University Press, Boston

© 1990 Massachusetts Historical Society

All Rights Reserved

❖❖❖❖❖

A Massachusetts Historical Society Bicentennial Book

Published at the Charge of the Publication Fund

❖❖❖❖❖

Library of Congress Cataloging-in-Publication Data

Tucker, Louis Leonard, 1927-
   Clio's consort: Jeremy Belknap and the founding of the Massachu-
setts Historical Society.
   Includes bibliographical references.
   ISBN 0-934909-27-X
   1. Belknap, Jeremy, 1744-1798. 2. Historians—Massachusetts—
Biography. 3. Congregational churches—Massachusetts—Clergy—
Biography. 4. Massachusetts Historical Society—History—18th cen-
tury. I. Title.
E175.5.B43T83   1990
973'.07202—dc20   89-37632

Printed by The Shagbark Press, South Portland, Maine

*This publication is presented in commemoration of
the bicentennial anniversary of the
Massachusetts Historical Society (1991).*

*It is respectfully dedicated to the staff of the
Massachusetts Historical Society
all consorts of Clio
who perpetuate Jeremy Belknap's standards of
excellence in scholarship
and share his commitment to the preservation
of America's historical resources.*

Contents

Acknowledgments

AS in the case of all authors, I was assisted by many as I developed this study. I am pleased to acknowledge their help, while absolving them of the responsibility of any errors contained therein.

The American Association for State and Local History awarded me a travel grant in 1985, which allowed me to conduct research in London and Edinburgh.

Professor Jere Daniell of the Department of History, Dartmouth College, provided helpful suggestions on chapters 1 and 2.

My son Assistant Professor Mark Tucker of the Department of Music, Columbia University, provided numerous suggestions for stylistic improvements in the manuscript.

A number of my colleagues on the Massachusetts Historical Society staff helped me in innumerable ways, particularly the late John Cushing, Malcolm Freiberg, Peter Drummey, Celeste Walker, Aimée Bligh—and the entire library staff.

I extend special thanks to the Society's editorial staff (Conrad E. Wright, Edward Hanson, Sheila Falcey) for their expert processing of the manuscript. I am especially grateful to Conrad E. Wright, Editor of Publications, for his solid professional judgments on such critical matters as organization and interpretation.

My Administrative Assistant, Donelle Meyer, typed and retyped and retyped numerous drafts, all the while maintaining her pleasant demeanor. If she grew tired of this subject, I can well understand her feeling.

Introduction

O N the evening of January 24, 1791, during the first administration of President George Washington, eight Bostonians met and founded "the Historical Society"; it was chartered and renamed "the Massachusetts Historical Society" in 1794. This was the first such organization established in the United States. The purposes of the founders were to collect, preserve, and publish the basic sources of American history: books, manuscripts, pamphlets, and the like. Their geographical focus was the entire nation, all 13 states, not just Massachusetts or New England.

All of these men had lived through the era of the American Revolution. They had been passionate patriots during the war and ardent nationalists when the republic was established. Filled with optimism, they foresaw a bright future for the young nation. Like George Berkeley, the bishop of Cloyne, they believed that "westward the course of the empire takes its way." They were eager to make their contribution to the development of what they conceived to be a new and dynamic political and social order in the world. An historical society would be a tangible contribution to the cause.

The moving force and principal founder of the Society was the Reverend Jeremy Belknap, a 47-year-old Congregational minister and a gifted historian. A longtime collector of documentary sources, Belknap came to realize that only through a formal organization, not through the efforts of individuals, could the study of American history be stimulated and developed to a high level. In this sense, he manifested the "spirit of the times." Following the Revolution, Americans (particularly New Englanders) established a multitude of institutions designed to do "good works."

This study recounts Belknap's pivotal role in the creation of the Society. Since the founding was inextricably linked to his activities as an historian, I have also discussed this aspect of his career. My focus, however, has not been on Belknap's historical writings, *per se*, but rather on his values as an historian. These were not conventional for this period. Belknap fervently believed that a work of history must not only be based upon the most authoritative primary sources but must also be factually accurate, as consistent with truth as was humanly possible to achieve. It could well be argued that Belknap was the founder of the "scientific history" movement in the United States.

While Belknap cannot be credited as a founder of the social sciences, he was one of its pioneer American practitioners, a counterpart to such 18th-century European intellectual luminaries as Montesquieu, Voltaire, Adam Smith, Edward Gibbon, and Adam Ferguson. Belknap, too, was an avid student of society and applied the principle of objective analysis to human activity. For him, history was more than a mere recording of what had transpired in the past. History offered insights into the creation and workings of human institutions and the nature of society.

Belknap was also one of America's earliest and leading cultural nationalists. Through his historical writings, in particular, he helped to stimulate the spirit of national pride in the first decades of the republic. The historical society he founded made a notable contribution in this effort.

I have carried the story of the Society to the time of Belknap's death in 1798 because his efforts in behalf of the institution during these formative years were as critical as his actions in founding it. Belknap was perceptive enough to realize that a grandiloquently phrased constitution was not in itself a sufficient base for a long-lived existence. The key to survival, in his judgment, was a sturdy physical foundation: a basic collection of historical materials. Substance must complement principles. Books and manuscripts must reinforce ideals.

After establishing the Society, Belknap worked diligently to lay this firm foundation. He was eminently successful. Without his conscientious efforts and energetic influence, the frail institution might have perished.

At this writing, nearly 200 years later, the Massachusetts Historical Society is a well-established institution and acknowledged to be one of the preeminent centers for historical research in the United States. A bicentennial commemoration is a proper time to recall how it all began.

Contemplate history . . . and what terms can adequately express its importance? If, with all the lights now reflected from experience, human existence be still in many respects a profound enigma, what would it not have been, with all these lights extinguished? Imagine, for a moment, all records of past events obliterated. Retain all other books and monuments, but let those of history be erased, expunged, annihilated—and then look around you. You see the fleeting present; you dimly guess, perhaps, at the doubtful future; but the PAST—the fixed, the mighty, the instructive past —what is it? All blank oblivion. Behind you stretches a dark, unknown, interminable gulf, which utterly severs you from the elder world. Across its still and sullen waters there comes no welcome voice, to greet you as brethren of the great human family which has passed away. All is dead silence, deep as of the grave. You know not who have lived before your time, nor what has been their fate. The chords of universal sympathy are shortened to a point. Your puny race commences with your own generation; and the precious memories of sixty centuries are lost to you forever. This great abstract idea has been clothed with a form which speaks forcibly to the eye. TIME has been represented as a gigantic, inexorable being, furnished with wings, and armed with a scythe: the one denoting his ceaseless flight, the other that he cuts down all before him. And such, in truth, would be his all-devastating career, were it not for HISTORY, which has likewise been embodied; and here you behold a still more powerful and majestic being, who grapples fearlessly with the giant Time, and wrests from his grasp the destroying scythe.

Timothy Walker,
"Annual Discourse, Delivered Before the Ohio Historical and Philosophical Society . . .",
Transactions of the Historical and Philosophical Society of Ohio, Part Second, I (1839): 181-182.

The work of the Massachusetts Historical Society is for the future far more than the present. There is no present. Only the past and the future count, the one interpreted for the benefit of the other.

Dixon Ryan Fox,
"Address at the Celebration of the One Hundred and Fiftieth Anniversary of the Massachusetts Historical Society," Mass. Hist. Soc., *Procs.,* 66 (1942): 422.

Biography

It has been my constant, habitual thought, ever since I was capable
of judging, that I should preach the gospel.

Jeremy Belknap [1766?]

TO one viewing the life of the Reverend Jeremy Belknap, the most
surprising development was his movement away from conventional expectations, both spiritually and in his ministerial career.[1]
Those 18th-century New Englanders who were raised in the tradition of moderate Calvinism usually remained consistent in their religious beliefs throughout their lives. Belknap, however, broke with
tradition and became an Arminian, a transition that would have distressed, perhaps scandalized, his conservative parents and parish
ministers had they been alive to witness it.

Belknap also followed an unconventional course in his professional career. For an 18th-century Congregational minister, pulpit
and parishioners were the sum and substance of life. Every waking
moment was to be devoted to pastoral duties and responsibilities.
And tradition held that the ministry was to be a lifelong commitment, once entered never to be left.

Not so in the case of Belknap. As the years passed, he began to
spend more of his time and mental energy on the researching and

---

1. My biographical account is heavily based on George B. Kirsch, *Jeremy
Belknap: A Biography* (New York, 1982); and Jane B. Marcou, *The Life of Jeremy Belknap, D.D.: The Historian of New Hampshire, With Selections From His
Correspondence and Other Writings* (New York, 1847). Marcou was Belknap's
granddaughter, and her book contains many extracts of family correspondence,
some of which has not survived. I also found valuable biographical data in the
following works: Clifford K. Shipton, *Sibley's Harvard Graduates*, 17 vols. to
date (Cambridge, Mass., and Boston, 1873-   ), 15:175-195; John Thornton Kirkland, *A Sermon Delivered at the Interment of Jeremy Belknap, D.D. . . . .* (Boston,
1798); and John Eliot, "Character of the Late Revd. Doctr. Belknap," in Transactions of the . . . Church in Long Lane, Federal Street Church Records, Massachusetts Historical Society, June 25, 1798. Belknap was christened Jeremiah, the
same name as his grandfather, but his parents adopted the shortened version,
Jeremy.

writing of history, his avocation. Soon his avocation came to take priority over his vocation. There were times when he seriously considered leaving the ministry and assuming a secular position.

In both respects, Belknap was not unique. He belonged to the advance guard of what subsequently became a broad movement in the religious history of Massachusetts. A few of Belknap's contemporaries followed a similar path. In the next generation, a host of New England clergymen not only joined the "migration" and embraced liberal Christianity but abandoned the ministry altogether. Some, like Jared Sparks and John Palfrey, became full-time historians, while others, like Ralph Waldo Emerson and Edward Everett, undertook other careers.

From birth until he completed his education and assumed his station in life as a minister, Belknap was a paragon of sound New England upbringing. Boston, the crucible of Massachusetts Puritanism, was his birthplace. The date was June 4, 1744, three decades before the crisis with Great Britain erupted. He was a fifth-generation British-American, the first Belknaps having arrived in New England in 1637 as part of the great Puritan migration.[2]

In the course of a century, the Belknap family achieved a modest respectability in Boston. They were typical middling Bostonians, pious, law-abiding, and industrious, and they exhibited a high degree of civic responsibility. They held minor public offices and were among the founders of Boston's storied Old South Church.[3]

Jeremy's parents upheld the family's reputation as solid citizens. His father, Joseph, a devout churchgoer, was a moderately successful tradesman. He began as a dresser and trader of leather and furs and later opened a shop in the front of his home to sell these items. Jeremy's mother, Sarah Byles, was linked to the Mather clan, one of the most honored families in early New England.[4] By marrying

2. For the genealogy of the Belknap family, see Marcou, *Belknap*, 9-10; and *New England Historical and Genealogical Register*, 68:83-92, 190-198 (1914).

3. On the early history of the church, see Benjamin Wisner, *The History of the Old South Church in Boston . . .* (Boston, 1830); Hamilton A. Hill, *History of the Old South Church [Third Church] Boston, 1669-1884* (Boston, 1890).

4. On this remarkable family, see Robert Middlekauff, *The Mathers: Three Generations of Puritan Intellectuals, 1596-1728* (New York, 1971).

Sarah, Joseph substantially elevated his own social standing. Both Joseph and Sarah conformed to a customary New England pattern that gave their children's lives a hue of predictability.

This was certainly so in the case of Jeremy, an intent and serious child. The parents "designed" their "beloved and only" son for the ministry, a common practice in colonial New England. "It has been my constant, habitual thought, ever since I was capable of judging," Jeremy wrote in later years, "that I should preach the gospel. With this view, my parents educated me, and to this my friends have often urged and persuaded me."[5] Groomed from birth for the pulpit, the dutiful son turned into the path his parents had laid out for him.

Joseph and Sarah Belknap provided their son with his first intensive religious instruction. The church supplemented and reinforced their teachings. The two ministers of the Old South Church, Joseph Sewall and Thomas Prince, especially the latter, were influential in shaping Belknap's religious outlook.[6] The special intensity of young Belknap's religious interest is revealed by a set of carefully organized notes he prepared of a sermon delivered by a visiting minister, "Dom Williams," in 1754.[7] Jeremy was then ten years of age.

Formal education was also essential to the training of a boy destined for the ministry. Young Jeremy had seven years of classical instruction at the Boston Latin School, then under the direction of the competent schoolmaster and stern disciplinarian John "Old Gaffer" Lovell.[8] In 1758, one month shy of his 15th birthday, he entered Harvard College. A diligent student, he applied himself to books

5. Quoted in Marcou, *Belknap*, 23.

6. Sewall was the son of Judge Samuel Sewall of Salem witchcraft fame. A Harvard graduate (1707), he became co-minister of the Old South in 1712. He was staunchly conservative in religious conviction and wielded considerable influence in Boston ministerial circles. He died in office in 1769 at the age of 80. See Shipton, *Sibley's Harvard Graduates*, 5: 376-393. Prince was ordained at the Old South in 1718 and spent 40 years there. He died in 1758. See *ibid.*, 341-368. See also Samuel G. Drake, *Some Memoirs of the Life and Writings of the Rev. Thomas Prince Together With a Pedigree of His Family* (Boston, 1851), esp. 3-10.

7. Marcou, *Belknap*, 10-11.

8. On Lovell, see Shipton, *Sibley's Harvard Graduates*, 8: 441-446.

and classroom exercises, avoided the "abominable lasciviousness" of his peers, and graduated in 1762.[9]

After graduating from Harvard, prospective ministers usually took employment as teachers in rural communities and, in their free time, "read divinity" with seasoned local clergymen.[10] Belknap followed this pattern. For nearly five years, he kept school in Milton, Massachusetts, and Portsmouth and Greenland, New Hampshire. During this period he studied with three ministers and preached occasionally as a "supply" in neighboring churches under the watchful eye of resident clergymen.

In 1765, while at Greenland, he took stock of his spiritual condition and found himself wanting, not an unusual circumstance for young ministerial candidates of that era. He bared his soul to his great-uncle Mather Byles,[11] a well-known Boston cleric and the grandson of Increase Mather, "the last American Puritan."[12] Belknap confessed that he had experienced "many agonies of the Soul." He was convinced that he was an unregenerate sinner and unfit to serve as an ambassador of God. "It is a fixed and settled opinion with me," he wrote, "that no Person ought to take on him the office of a minister of the Gospel unless he has experienced the renovating Power of it on his own Soul—but unhappy me, I have never experienced this and therefore I dare not preach tho' I have been much urged to it."[13]

9. On student problems at 18th-century Harvard, see Samuel Eliot Morison, *Three Centuries of Harvard, 1636-1936* (Cambridge, Mass., 1936), ch. 6 and *passim*; "Benjamin Wadsworth's Book, 1725-1736," Colonial Society of Massachusetts, *Publications*, 31 (1935): 452-458.

10. The grooming of a Puritan minister is comprehensively examined in Mary L. Gambrell, *Ministerial Training in Eighteenth-Century New England* (New York, 1937).

11. See Arthur W. H. Eaton, *The Famous Mather Byles, the Noted Boston Tory Preacher, Poet and Wit, 1707-1788* (Boston, 1914). Byles was also the great-grandson of Richard Mather and John Cotton. Clifford Shipton described the colorful Byles as "the poet laureate and the official literary greeter of the province" and "the greatest wit of his day." See Byles's biographical sketch in *Sibley's Harvard Graduates*, 7: 464-493.

12. See Michael G. Hall, *The Last American Puritan: The Life of Increase Mather, 1639-1723* (Middletown, 1988).

13. Belknap to Byles, Sept. 5, 1765, Belknap Papers, Massachusetts Historical Society.

Belknap could not muster the courage to tell his parents of his decision. He was acutely sensitive to the impact such news would have upon them. He therefore asked Byles to inform his parents of his decision "in such a manner as you think most proper." Byles assured "My Dear Child" that his self-doubts were understandable, and that he should not be so harsh upon himself: "God, who sees your infirmities, sees also your resistance, your agonies, your repentances."[14] Byles urged him to stay his course.

Notwithstanding Byles's reassuring words, Belknap continued to experience a crisis of conscience. Throughout 1765, as the Stamp Act controversy swirled over New England, Belknap remained locked in the grip of his personal spiritual dilemma. The conscientious young man gave serious thought to abandoning ministerial studies and devoting his life to teaching the "poor aborigines" at Eleazar Wheelock's Indian School in Lebanon, Connecticut.[15] A friend and former Harvard classmate sought to dissuade him from this notion, reminding him of his parents' expectation that "in proper time [he would] undertake the blessed work of preaching the gospel," and that any other occupation would "rather give them pain than pleasure. You can hardly imagine how their comfort depends on you, and how they are grieved when your desires counteract their judgement."[16]

Then, in 1766, suddenly and dramatically, young Belknap experienced conversion and the anguish vanished, replaced by inward peace: "A glorious discovery of the riches and freeness of divine grace, and the infinite worthiness of the Lord Jesus Christ which I trust was made to my soul by the Holy Spirit, at once changed my views and dispositions; and from that time I devoted myself to the service of God in the gospel of his Son, thinking it my duty to glorify God in this way."[17] Believing he possessed the gift of God's grace, he renewed his ministerial studies.

14. Quoted in Marcou, *Belknap*, 17.

15. Wheelock to Belknap, Greenland, May 31, 1766, Mass. Hist. Soc., *Coll.*, 6th ser., 4:8-9. On Wheelock's Indian School experiment, see James McCallum, *Eleazar Wheelock: Founder of Dartmouth College* (Hanover, 1939), ch. 4, *passim*.

16. Quoted in Marcou, *Belknap*, 23.

17. *Ibid.*, 24.

In the winter of 1767, the First Parish of Dover, New Hampshire, called Belknap as its junior pastor. Its senior minister, the Reverend Jonathan Cushing, was old and sickly and could no longer carry out his responsibilities.[18] Out of compassion the parish retained Cushing in nominal leadership.

For a 22-year-old novice this was a promising assignment; Belknap quickly accepted the offer.[19] Organized in 1633, ten years after the town's founding, the First Church was the oldest in the colony. Its first six ministers had been graduates of Cambridge University and the next four, including Cushing, had been educated at Harvard. Cushing had assumed the Dover pulpit in 1717 and was in his 50th year of service when Belknap arrived. Cushing had enjoyed a successful ministry and was popular with his parishioners. Belknap found him to be a "grave and sound preacher; a kind, peaceable, prudent, and judicious pastor, a wise and faithful friend . . . a large, stout man."[20]

Belknap was ordained in February 1767 and promptly became the functional minister.[21] He assumed full control when the 79-year-old Cushing died on March 25, 1769.

After graduating from Harvard, Belknap welcomed the opportunity to exchange the hurly burly of Boston for the serenity and slow-paced world of rural New England. While teaching in Greenland, he had been offered a similar position in Boston but rejected it. As he informed the town clerk, who extended the offer: "A quiet and comfortable country life is the greatest temporal happiness that I wish to enjoy, and I am perfectly contented with my present situation."[22]

Dover, too, offered Belknap a serene country setting.[23] Situated

18. On Cushing, see Shipton, *Sibley's Harvard Graduates*, 5: 634-635. For the history of the church, see *The First Parish in Dover, New Hampshire* (Dover, 1884); this publication commemorated the 250th anniversary of the church.

19. Documents relating to Belknap's appointment can be seen in Mass. Hist. Soc., *Coll.*, 6th ser., 4: 10-23.

20. Quoted in Shipton, *Sibley's Harvard Graduates*, 5: 635.

21. Rev. Samuel Haven, *A Sermon Preached February 18, 1767 at the Ordination of Jeremy Belknap* (Portsmouth, 1767).

22. Quoted in Marcou, *Belknap*, 19.

23. On the early history of Dover, see John Scales, *History of Dover, New Hampshire*, 2 vols. (Manchester, 1932), vol. 1; John Scales, ed., *Historical Mem-

on the Cocheco River in the midst of rolling hills, Dover was a pic-
turesque town. Although it still bore the coarse physical appearance
of a frontier settlement, it was a community on the rise. When Belknap arrived, it had a population of slightly more than 1,600, which
made it New Hampshire's fourth largest settlement. It was experiencing rapid growth and exhibited a vibrant commercial spirit. Lum-
bering was the mainstay of its economy with agriculture also important. While located at the edge of the forest primeval, Dover was
not too distant from larger settlements. Portsmouth, New Hampshire's principal city and a bustling seaport of 4,400, was a mere 10
miles to the southwest, and Boston was only 66 miles away.

Belknap enjoyed his new surroundings at first, but within a few
years he became less enamored of the bucolic charm of country life
and began to yearn for the cultural and cosmopolitan setting of
Boston. Much of his discontent stemmed from his ministry, which
proved to be an abysmal failure. Belknap began his clerical career
with ambitious plans. With a zeal characteristic of the young, he
threw himself into his chosen profession. In an effort to revitalize
what he perceived to be a theologically complacent congregation, he
sought to impose rigid orthodox standards for baptism and church
membership, as, for example, the necessity of a conversion experience.[24] At this early stage of his career, Belknap clung to conservative religious tenets. His parishioners had no desire to return to the
rigid, old-time religion, however, and resisted his efforts. Tensions
soon developed between minister and congregation. Within a few
years, as the opposition intensified and Belknap came to recognize
that he was fighting a lost cause, his passion for reform began to
wane and his ministry settled into monotonous, if not tedious, rou-
tine.

Closely connected to Belknap's waning enthusiasm for the clerical
life were his financial difficulties. Four months after his ordination,
he returned to Boston and married Ruth Eliot, the daughter of a

oranda *Concerning Persons and Places in Old Dover, New Hampshire* (Dover,
1900); Jeremy Belknap, *The History of New Hampshire*, 3 vols. (Philadelphia
and Boston, 1784-1792), vol. 1, *passim*; George Wadleigh, *Notable Events in the
History of Dover, New Hampshire* (Dover, 1913).

24. On Belknap's efforts for reform, see Kirsch, *Belknap*, 28-30.

bookseller.[25] In the next 11 years the couple produced six children.[26] As his family increased, Belknap needed additional income. But his parishioners failed to respond. Indeed, some years they did not even provide him with his regular salary, much less an increase. The failure to receive a steady stipend, together with the raging inflation and rapid depreciation of currency provoked by wartime economic conditions, kept Belknap impoverished. At one point, he considered selling his house to pay off old debts.

During the final decade of his residence in Dover, Belknap locked horns with his congregation, essentially over the salary issue,[27] but the sources of friction were much deeper than dollars. The dispute degenerated into an acrimonious squabble, with each side hurling invectives at one another. While bitter battles between Congregational ministers and parishioners were commonplace in 18th-century New England, the Belknap-First Church controversy achieved a special notoriety because of its long duration.[28]

With each passing year Belknap became increasingly disenchanted with the ministry and further alienated from his parishioners. While he continued to perform his multifarious pastoral duties, he did so in a perfunctory manner. His spirits sank lower and lower, and he came to lead a life of "quiet desperation." As he wrote of his finan-

25. Belknap made these laconic entries in his diary relative to his trip to Boston to get married: "June 12. Set out for Boston, lodged at North Hill. 13. Travelled to Ipswich met Governor Wentworth on the Road he entered Portsmouth this day. 14. Preached at Ipswich. 15. reached Boston evening *married*. 18. Set out on our Return, rode through the Rain, and lodged at Hampton, Mr. Thayer's. 19. Got home to Dover in evening safe and well." Belknap, Diaries, Massachusetts Historical Society.

26. Sarah, born Apr. 7, 1768; Joseph, born Dec. 2, 1769; Samuel, born Dec. 31, 1771; Elizabeth, born Apr. 3, 1774; John, born Dec. 30, 1776; Andrew, born June 4, 1779.

27. Because it was an issue of enormous importance to him, Belknap not only preserved the original documents bearing upon his problems with the church officials, but he also made copies of them. Many of these documents have been printed in Mass. Hist. Soc., *Coll.*, 6th ser., 4: 342-379, *passim*.

28. Belknap's case is discussed in Charles C. Smith, "Financial Embarrassments of the New England Ministries in the Last Century," American Antiquarian Society, *Proceedings*, new ser., 7 (1890): 129-135. See also, George B. Kirsch, "Clerical Dismissals in Colonial and Revolutionary New Hampshire," *Church History*, 49 (1980): 160-177.

cial problems and parish dispute in 1779: "These things are a continual source of vexation both of body and mind; they take off my attention from my proper business, and unfit me for the duties of my station."[29]

What had gone wrong? Why did Belknap fail in his ministry? There were ostensibly many reasons. It could be argued, for example, that he was miscast as a minister. His primary interest was in secular matters of the mind, not theology or servicing the spiritual needs of parishioners. His natural habitat was the study, not the pulpit. Family influence and tradition had led him into the ministry, and expediency and financial necessity kept him there, even though it became manifestly apparent that he was neither emotionally nor temperamentally suited for such a career.

As for the difficulties Belknap experienced with his parishioners during his last decade in Dover, his problems were not unique. The fact is that minister-congregation relationships were always a delicate matter in 18th-century New England. There was a conspicuous intellectual and social gap between a minister, who was a college graduate, and his flock. Most clergymen were able to bridge this gap and maintain friendly, if not harmonious, relations with their parishioners. There were some, however, who were not able to achieve rapport and eventually became embroiled in nasty conflicts.

Belknap was among this latter group. Haughty in personality and possessing strong intellectual proclivities, he found it difficult to socialize with his flock on an equal footing. Like a patriarch of the past, he stood aloof from his congregation, especially those who comprised the rank and file. By assuming this lofty stance, he compounded his problems.[30] As his most recent biographer has noted,

29. Quoted in Marcou, *Belknap*, 121. On Dec. 11, 1781, an angry and frustrated Belknap wrote his parish: "Since I lived in this town I never was reduced so low at this season of the year, nor so destitute of the common necessaries of life as now. Have you any intention to provide me with the necessary means of subsistence, or do you design to wear out my patience and reduce me to despair?" Quoted in Mass. Hist. Soc. *Procs.*, 2nd ser., 4 (1887-1889): 206.

30. I am greatly indebted to Professor Jere R. Daniell of the Dartmouth College History Department for clarifying my thoughts on the critical issue of Belknap's problems with his parishioners. Daniell is a key authority on the early history of New Hampshire.

his "inability to communicate on a close personal level with many of the townspeople explains much of his trouble over his two decades as the town minister."[31]

Belknap particularly failed as a communicator in the pulpit, a serious drawback for a minister. Eighteenth-century New England Congregationalism produced a host of charismatic sermonizers, like "silver-tongued" Samuel Cooper of the Brattle Street Church,[32] but Belknap was not among this elite group. While the Reverend Ezra Stiles noted in his diary that he had heard Belknap preach an "excellent Sermon, Acts—Almost thou persuadest me to be Christian,"[33] other ministers who listened to him on a regular basis reported that he was not stimulating, much less mesmeric. One of his friends wrote: "His prayers in public were but little varied and he was almost motionless in the pulpit. Scarcely did he appear even to move his lips."[34] The minister who delivered Belknap's funeral sermon described his prosaic preaching in these diplomatic words: "His preaching was designed to make you good and happy, and not to gain your applause. Whilst the manner as well as matter was suited to affect the heart, no attempt was made to overbear your imaginations and excite your passions by clamorous and affected tones."[35] In short, he was a dull preacher. This, too, did not endear him to his disaffected parishioners.

Belknap's failure to achieve theological reform in the First Church can be attributed in some measure to his misreading of the temper

31. Kirsch, *Belknap*, 17.

32. Charles Akers, *The Divine Politician: Samuel Cooper and the American Revolution in Boston* (Boston, 1982), 23. Cooper's singular preaching style is discussed on 20-24.

33. Franklin Dexter, ed., *The Literary Diary of Ezra Stiles*, 3 vols. (New York, 1901), 3:190.

34. Dr. John Peirce, quoted in Samuel A. Eliot, "Jeremy Belknap: A Paper in Recognition of the One Hundred and Fiftieth Anniversary of the Massachusetts Historical Society," Mass. Hist. Soc., *Procs.*, 66 (1936-1941): 99.

35. Kirkland, *Sermon at Interment of Belknap*, 14. A 20th-century minister of Belknap's church, who was related to Jeremy's wife, made this assessment of Belknap's sermonizing: "From his printed sermons that survive I cannot believe that he was a stirring preacher. I am afraid that his discourses, judged by a modern sermon-taster, might justify the familiar heading of a stockmarket report, 'firm but dull.'" See Eliot, "Belknap," 99.

of the times. Dramatic changes had taken place in rural New England after the Revolution. Thousands of emigrants from the coastal area, in search of greater economic opportunity, had moved into the newly opened lands of Maine, New Hampshire, Vermont, and the Berkshire hills. The villages and towns of the northern and western frontier suddenly began to experience growing pains. The swelling of population produced social tensions and pressures on the land supply. Social unrest and economic problems provoked political controversy. The days of close-knit, tightly controlled settlements basking in harmony, unity, and order were over. Pluralism replaced homogeneity.[36]

The changes in religion were especially significant. Baptists, Quakers, Shakers, Universalists, and other "radicals" swarmed into the hill country, organized churches, and soon challenged the monolithic authority of the established Congregational Church.[37] These sects added numerous converts after the Great Awakening of the 1740s when the once all-powerful Congregational Church began to crumble. The apostates from Congregationalism repudiated the harsh tenets of New England Calvinism and joined the ranks of the dissenting sects.

Dover was a microcosm of what was transpiring throughout rural New England. A growing number of Baptists and Quakers moved into the town, established churches, and stood as challengers to the once-dominant First Parish. Unfortunately for Belknap, these developments coincided with his ministry. He failed to comprehend the consequences of the changes Dover was experiencing. His vision was myopic. His program of reform was ill-advised and doomed to failure.

It is ironic to note that, in the course of his nearly 20-year stay in Dover, especially in the final decade, Belknap underwent a marked change in his own theological orientation, although it had no bear-

36. In recent years, a number of scholars have examined this subject. See, for example, Michael Zuckerman, *Peaceable Kingdoms: New England Towns in the Eighteenth Century* (New York, 1970); Kenneth A. Lockridge, "Social Change and the Meaning of the American Revolution," *Journal of Social History*, 6 (1973): 403-439.

37. This topic is analyzed in Stephen Marini, *Radical Sects of Revolutionary New England* (Cambridge, Mass., 1982).

ing on his ministerial activities at the First Church. That change is revealed only in his personal writings, principally in letters to close friends. In his sermons, public pronouncements, and printed works, he professed the standard Westminster Calvinism of his youthful days in Boston and his first years as a minister. He espoused the conservative religious doctrines of his pious parents, the Reverend Messrs. Prince and Sewall, and the Congregational establishment.

In his private writings, however, Belknap displayed the rationalist tendencies of his age, the religious liberalism of the Enlightenment. He began to question and, in some instances, reject the principal tenets of the orthodox faith, from original sin to predestination to the necessity of conversion for church membership. The moderate Calvinist quietly metamorphosed into a liberal or Arminian. He moved steadily in the direction of what subsequently became Unitarianism.[38]

While Belknap was careful to keep his liberal theological views private, he openly espoused liberal sentiments in a number of non-doctrinal areas. For example, he displayed a remarkable tolerance for differing religious points of view, within a Protestant framework, to be sure; his toleration did not extend to Catholics, Jews, or even Quakers. As he informed Ebenezer Hazard[39] of Philadelphia in 1784:

38. See Kirsch, *Belknap*, chs. 2, 9, *passim*. Conrad Wright, in his seminal study, *The Beginnings of Unitarianism in America* (Boston, 1955), regards Belknap as an "Arminian" and proto-Unitarian. See p. 252, *passim*.

39. Born in 1744, Hazard was a native of Philadelphia, a graduate of the College of New Jersey (1762), a publisher and bookseller in New York City from 1769 to 1775, and was serving as "Surveyor of the Post Roads throughout the U.S." when he met Belknap in 1778 while traveling through New England. An avid historian, and collector (and transcriber) of documents and printed historical sources, Hazard sought to publish a collection of American state papers. As he wrote Jonathan Trumbull: "I wish to be the means of saving from oblivion many important papers which without something like this collection will infallibly be lost. . . . [Some papers] are intimately connected with the liberties of the people; others will furnish some future historian with valuable materials. The time will doubtless come when early periods of American history will be eagerly inquired into, and it is the duty of every generation to hand to its successor the necessary means of acquiring such knowledge, in order to prevent their groping in the dark, and perplexing themselves in the labrinths of error." Quoted in Shelly, "Ebenezer Hazard," 48, cited below.

Belknap and Hazard became fast friends and developed one of the more notable exchanges of correspondence following the Revolution. It covered a period

"I desire to hold communion with good people of every Christian denomination, let their opinions on speculative points or ritual institutions be ever so different from my own. For this, I suppose, some gentlemen stigmatize me with the name of a *'Latitudinarian'*; but, if I err, I had rather err on the side of catholicism than of bigotry."[40]

Belknap also refused to become enmeshed in local or regional religious controversies (exclusive of those in which he was a principal). He had a strong distaste for polemical religion and refused to argue and denounce. He could not hide his impatience with those clerical colleagues who regularly flayed each other in print. Nor would he participate in church councils which were convened to examine the principles of fellow clergy. As he wrote in 1783 to the town of Wakefield's church officials, who had asked him to serve on such a council: "No one who has been acquainted with ecclesiastical history can help knowing that the calling of Councils to judge and determine articles of faith has been of the most pernicious consequence to the true interest of religion."[41]

Belknap's dislike of controversial theology was apparently deeply rooted. In 1769, a young Harvard graduate who was preparing for the ministry asked Belknap for advice in his studies. He responded:

Divinity is not the art of disputing about divine truth, nor of puzzling yourself and others with metaphysical subtleties; but it is the knowledge of God and Christ, and the Gospel. And where is this to be found, but in the revelation which God has made to the world? To these pure and unerring oracles, I would direct you; there you may search for and receive divine truth, without the least suspicion of being deceived, provided you come with an humble, meek, and teachable soul, as a new-born babe desiring the sincere milk of the word, etc.

of about 20 years. The Massachusetts Historical Society published two volumes of their correspondence in 1877 (Mass. Hist. Soc., *Coll.*, 5th ser., vols. 2 and 3). These works have been a cornucopia of historical information for modern scholars and an invaluable source for this study. On Hazard, see Fred Shelly, "Ebenezer Hazard: America's First Historical Editor," *William and Mary Quarterly*, 3rd ser., 12:44-73 (1955); Mass. Hist. Soc., *Coll.*, 5th ser., 2: preface, x-xii.

40. Belknap to Hazard, Dover, Apr. 11, 1784, *ibid.*, 326.

41. *Ibid.*, 6th ser., 4:255. The entire document is on 253-257. Here and throughout this book I have modernized quotations by expanding contractions, rendering ampersands as "and," and bringing superscripts down to the line.

But, if you make systematical and polemical authors your chief study, you will be in danger of having your mind turned away from the simplicity of the Gospel, and of being led into some scheme of religion that will be set up as an idol in your heart, and be made use of as a standard to try all other opinions by.[42]

In 1780, Belknap delivered a sermon based upon John 18. A listener took umbrage over his doctrinal interpretation and "printed a piece" in which he flogged the minister "severely." Belknap refused to respond to the diatribe. Sixteen years later (!) the critic wrote Belknap and demanded an answer to his charges: "Now if you was right, I have done very wrong, and it is expedient that my piece should be answered, if capable of an answer: therefore, if you are able, you will kindly undertake an answer, or to show the error. Otherwise, my cause is established, and you are found in an egregious deception."

Belknap was finally constrained to respond to his captious critic: "If Mr. S. is disposed to enter into controversy, he is very unfortunate in the choice of an antagonist; for if his performance has passed sixteen years without a reply, it is not probable that it will receive any at this distance of time, when both that and the sermon which gave occasion for it, are almost forgotten. Those who have read them can judge for themselves."[43]

Belknap eloquently expressed his religious (and philosophical) liberalism in a letter to Hazard in 1784:

Suppose at the time of the institution of the Royal Society . . . there had been a scheme of Philosophy drawn from Aristotle, Descartes, Rohault, or some other writers that were then in vogue, containing what the Society thought the true systems of nature, and it had been made a standing order that no man should be admitted a member, but those that would subscribe it, or declare their assent to it. How would such a term of admission consist with the design of such a society which is to enquire into, and make

42. Quoted in Marcou, *Belknap*, 39. The minister who delivered Belknap's funeral sermon described the content of his preaching in these words: "Your attention was never drawn from the great practical views of the gospel by the needless introduction of controversial subjects; nor your minds perplexed, nor your devotional feelings damped by the cold subtleties of metaphysick." Kirkland, *Sermon at Interment of Belknap*, 14.

43. The exchange is printed in Marcou, *Belknap*, 224.

discoveries in, natural philosophy? Would it not be a *bar* to enquiries? How could our modern improvements be reconciled to those old defective and exploded principles? To apply this remark. The book of Nature and the book of Scripture, being works of the same Author, are open to the inspection of all men, and our business is to search them, and learn what we can of them. If it is the business of a philosopher *freely* to enquire into the works of the Creator, it is equally that of the divine *freely* to enquire into the word of God. . . . But creeds, either in philosophy or divinity, should never be imposed, because they tend to fetter the mind and stop its genuine excursions into the field of truth. For this reason I have long since utterly discarded all confessions or standards of human authority.[44]

The First Church parishioners were not exposed to the liberal Belknap. They encountered a stern taskmaster who clung to high moral and ethical standards and insisted that his flock do likewise. If they committed indiscretions, they felt the sharp sting of his tongue as well as his pen.

Belknap's displeasure with Dover transcended his parish to the community at large. Possessing a speculative mind, he was intensely interested in cultural and intellectual matters, but, in his judgment, Dover was barren of the arts of gentle life and its citizens did not conduct a brisk commerce in ideas. He did not regard the town as the ideal site for intellectual adventurers. Boston remained his spiritual home and point of reference.

In 1783, Belknap delivered a scathing indictment of his adopted town and its uncultured citizens in a letter to Hazard:

I have long thought, and do still think it one of the greatest misfortunes of my life to be obliged to rear a family of children in a place and among a people where insensibility to the interests of the rising generation, and an inveterate antipathy to literature, are to be reckoned among the prevailing vices; where there is not so much public spirit as to build a school-house; where men of the first rank let their children grow up uncultivated as weeds in the highway; where grand jurors pay no regard to their oaths; and where a judge on the bench has publicly instructed them to invent

44. Belknap to Hazard, Dover, Apr. 11, 1784, Mass. Hist. Soc., *Coll.*, 5th ser., 2: 324-325.

subterfuges and evasions to cheat their consciences and prevent the execution of the laws for the advancement of learning.[45]

Hazard shared one of Belknap's diatribes against the Dover citizenry with some friends and later informed him: "They were astonished and as much hurt as myself at the thought that a man of your genius and education should be doomed to drag out a miserable existence among such savages."[46]

Belknap brooded and sank into "the glooms" in Dover.[47] A vibrant intellectual with an "insatiable curiosity," he had an absorbing passion for books and knowledge. These were his Elysium. He craved contact with men of similar interests, but they were not to be found in "the semi-barbarous region of the North," as he once described his place of residence.[48] Table talk there was of the here and now, never some remote realm of ideas. Increasingly, he felt like an exile and intellectual recluse, cut off from the world of thought. Like Jonathan Swift in Ireland, he, too, looked upon himself as "a stranger in a strange land."

Winters were especially trying for Belknap. The severe weather caused a reduction in travel and curtailed postal deliveries. All mail had to be hand-delivered from Portsmouth since Dover did not have a post office. As his contacts with the outside world shriveled, his

45. Mass. Hist. Soc., *Coll.*, 5th ser., 2:287-288. At another time, Belknap illustrated the cultural limitations of the Dover citizenry in this manner. He circulated a proposal for subscriptions to his *History of New Hampshire* and prices for individual copies were "in sheets," "in boards," or "bound." Some Doverites, who were more acquainted with lumber than with books, thought that "in boards" meant that payment could be made with lumber. Wrote Belknap: "I was obliged to shew them a book stitched and covered in the form I expected this would be, and tell them, as I would a child, that the boards mentioned were pasteboard with which the book was to be covered, and not pine boards received for the pay. Thus you have a specimen of Dover. How it will be understood, or what effect it will have in other parts of this ignorant wooden world, I know not." Belknap to Hazard, Dover, June 23, 1783, *ibid.*, 221-222.

46. Hazard to Belknap, Philadelphia, Jan. 16, 1784, *ibid.*, 298.

47. "Why so much in the glooms?" John Eliot (writing from Boston) inquired on July 31, 1781. *Ibid.*, 6th ser., 4:210-211. Eliot wrote that "it is part of [Belknap's wife's] duty to keep you out of the dumps."

48. Belknap to Hazard, Dover, Feb. 2, 1787, *ibid.*, 5th ser., 2:455. Belknap also asserted that the bustling port city of Portsmouth was a cultural wasteland. He said that there were not more than a dozen "readers" in the city.

moroseness and sense of isolation grew. It was now time to burrow down and read. As winter began in 1784, he informed Hazard: "I am now *denned* like the bears till next April, but have taken care to lay in a stock of literary fodder." The fodder included the 4-volume edition of Samuel Johnson's *Lives of the Poets* and the 16-volume edition of Rollin's *Roman History*, which "will enable me to chew the cud through a great part of the ensuing winter."[49]

Belknap's correspondence is filled with melancholy statements about his cultural isolation. "I think I ought to make an apology to you for asking so many questions and favours of you," he wrote in 1785 to Hazard, "but, when you recollect that I am placed in such a sequestered spot, and have so little communication with the world, and yet have an insatiable curiosity, and, I hope, an *honest* desire to do things right, you will form the apology yourself."[50] Belknap bewailed his lack of time to pursue intellectual studies: " 'Confined', as Pope says, 'to lead the life of a cabbage,'—unable to stir from the spot where I am planted; burdened with the care of an increasing family, and obliged to pursue the proper business of my station,— I have neither time nor advantages to make any improvements in science."[51] He longed to visit a "*centre* of science in America, and rub off the rust contracted in this obscurity."[52]

Above all, he lamented the lack of stimulating conversations. A clubbable man, he longed for intellectual companionship. To John Eliot, a Boston minister and his wife's cousin, he confided: "I constantly feel the want of such a friend as you are to converse with, and especially when I meet with any difficulty or any new thought pops into my head which I want to turn round and round and examine inch by inch, as I think every thing ought to be before it is admitted for truth in speculation or made a rule of conduct."[53] In a

49. Belknap to Hazard, Dover, Nov. 16, 1784, *ibid.*, 3: 373[25].

50. Belknap to Hazard, Dover, Feb. 11, 1785, *ibid.*, 2: 414-415.

51. Belknap to Hazard, Dover, May 12, 1779, *ibid.*, 6.

52. Belknap to Hazard, Dover, Aug. 28, 1780, *ibid.*, 69.

53. Belknap to Eliot, [Dover], Dec. 5, 1781, *ibid.*, 6th ser., 4: 219. Eliot relished the isolation Belknap was lamenting. He wrote: "I wish to exchange situations with you for a little while. I am tired to death of company,—those in whose company there is neither profit or entertainment." Eliot to Belknap, Boston, Sept. 5, 1781, *ibid.*, 217.

similar vein, he informed Hazard: "Nothing would please me better
than to be your fellow-traveller, in quest of natural curiosities."[54]
He was envious of Hazard who was then moving to Philadelphia,
where he would soon be "revelling in the full luxury of scientific
entertainment, you must think sometimes of your poor friend, starv-
ing in these forlorn regions, and let him have now and then a crum
from your table."[55]

In his journey to the western islands of Scotland in 1774, Samuel
Johnson met a culturally inclined "country gentleman" in a remote
area. Johnson expressed sorrow for such people because "they had
not enough to keep their minds in motion."[56] Belknap suffered a
similar fate in rural New Hampshire.

By 1786, Belknap knew that his days in Dover were numbered.
While there was no organized attempt being made to remove him,
his critics were numerous and vociferous. Nor was he held in favor
by his parish leaders. He was acutely aware that he could no longer
function effectively as the spiritual leader of this church. A future
there was continued misery and frustration. He must leave. In a revealing, "secret" letter to Hazard, he wrote: "My principal concern
is to be usefully employed in such a way as shall not be a hinderance
to literary improvement, and to provide a decent maintenance and
proper education for my family. These latter cannot be had here, nor
is it possible for me here to indulge that strong relish for the conversation of men of sense and learning, which has been growing upon
me for years. Should I remove, there is no certainty that I shall prefer settling again in the same employment. The *indelible character*
does not appear in the same light to me as to many others. But this
I am certain of, that I shall prefer some capital town to those rural
scenes with which I was so delighted in my younger years, and a return to my native place would be extreemly eligible."[57]

Hazard made a persuasive effort to lure Belknap to Philadelphia.
He offered assistance in securing a combination of positions which

54. Belknap to Hazard, [Dover], Mar. 13, 1780, *ibid.*, 5th ser., 2:40.

55. Belknap to Hazard, Dover, Aug. 28, 1780, *ibid.*, 74.

56. *Johnson's Journey to the Western Islands of Scotland and Boswell's
Journal of a Tour to the Hebrides with Samuel Johnson, LL.D.*, ed. R. W. Chap-
man (London, 1970), 278.

57. [Dover], [1786?], Mass. Hist. Soc., *Coll.*, 5th ser., 2:429.

would provide his friend with a livable income: editor of an historical and literary journal; "Keeper of the Library in Carpenter's Hall"; and minister of a local church.[58] A friend in Boston urged Belknap to return to that city and begin a classical school, but he rejected the idea, affirming that he was not suited to teaching.

This was the nadir of Belknap's personal and professional life. He was forlorn, disillusioned, dispirited. He was 42 years old, on the verge of unemployment after devoting his prime years to an unsatisfying and unsuccessful ministry, and financially strapped with a large family to support.

Earning a livelihood for his family now became his paramount concern. But how could he achieve this objective? He had few options. The ministry was not a promising avenue. There was little prospect of securing a pulpit that would provide a high degree of financial security. With the exception of the affluent Brattle Street Church of Boston ("one of the great churches in the British Empire"),[59] few parishes in New England, Congregational or otherwise, compensated their ministers at a liberal level. Clerics commanded a large measure of respect but earned little hard cash. And what if he were to take another church and become ensnared in a repeat of the Dover experience? Did he really wish to remain a minister? Should he leave the church and begin a new life as an editor or teacher, professions which offered the promise of more leisure time for his scholarly activities? Should he pursue Hazard's plan and settle in Philadelphia? In September 1785, Belknap visited the Pennsylvania city and met many of its literati. They urged him to relocate.[60] He was impressed by the city, its residents, and its rich cultural mosaic.

After an intense internal struggle, Belknap concluded, however, that his best course of action was to remain in the ministry and in New England. From his perspective, the acme would have been a

58. A number of Hazard's letters to Belknap in 1786 and early 1787 dealt with employment opportunities in Philadelphia. See, for example, Hazard to Belknap, New York, Jan. 20, 1787, *ibid.*, 449-453.

59. The judgment of Charles Akers. See *Samuel Cooper*, 17.

60. In the preceding year, through the influence of Hazard, the American Philosophical Society elected Belknap an "honorary member" (i.e., a corresponding member). See Hazard to Belknap, Philadelphia, Jan. 24, 1784, Mass. Hist. Soc., *Coll.*, 5th ser., 2:300-306. Belknap's trip to Philadelphia, which was part of a seven-week sojourn, is recounted in Marcou, *Belknap*, 107-119.

well-established church in Boston, but the prospects for such an assignment were nil. A leading church in Boston would not select a minister with his record. He was fully aware of this.

Before Belknap could begin the search for a new pulpit, he had to sever his ties with the First Church. This was not easy. Custom dictated that a minister serve a parish until taken by death or struck down by a disabling illness. He had to obtain a formal dismission or dissolution of his contract in order to terminate the relationship. "The etiquette of removing a minister from a parish in New England," Belknap informed Hazard, "is as tedious as obtaining a divorce in the spiritual courts; and I am now in the worst part of it, viz., consulting and debating and waiting the answer of the parish to a proposal which I have made, either for *their* formal dismission of me or the calling a council."[61]

After a series of lengthy, tense meetings with church officials, Belknap secured the release from his contract. He was now "dismissed" and free to seek a new church.[62] "Never was I in such an unsettled state since you knew me," he wrote Hazard a few days after dissolving his relationship with the church, "and now more so am I than ever. . . . When shall I again feel settled?"[63]

Belknap began the time-consuming process of competing for open pulpits in Boston and the outlying area. He was offered a position in Beverly, just to the north of Boston, but for unknown reasons rejected it. He nearly secured a church in Exeter, New Hampshire, a post he coveted, but the congregation ultimately selected another candidate. He grew weary of the constant travel and solitary existence. "I could take up my chest and march at any time," he wrote Hazard, "and feel as happy in one place as another; but, having been so long used to a settled life, it is irksome to *be obliged* to be on the pad."[64]

In January 1787, there was a positive turn. Belknap received a "call" from the Long Lane Church in Boston, where he had preached

61. Belknap to Hazard, Dover, June 21, 1786, Mass. Hist. Soc., *Coll.*, 5th ser., 2:440.

62. *Ibid.*, 6th ser., 4:378-379.

63. Belknap to Hazard, Portsmouth, Sept. 27, 1786, *ibid.*, 5th ser., 2:443.

64. Belknap to Hazard, Dover, Oct. 25, 1786, Mass. Hist. Soc., *ibid.*, 444.

as a supply for nearly three months.[65] Long Lane was a church with an unusual history.[66] It was founded in 1730 by a doughty band of Scotch Presbyterians under the leadership of a dynamic, 23-year-old minister named John Moorhead. Born near Belfast, Ireland, and trained for the ministry at Glasgow University, Moorhead emigrated to America in 1729, taking up residence in Philadelphia. When the Presbytery there refused to honor his certificate of ordination, he struck out for Boston.

After settling there, Moorhead became affiliated with the Presbytery of Londonderry, New Hampshire, whose members had long sought to establish a religious beachhead in Congregational Boston. Moorhead became their point man. He converted a large barn into a meeting house, adding a steeple and bell tower and cutting a line of windows on both sides of the structure. He began his congregation with 30 members, some of whom had moved to Boston from Londonderry. In two years, he increased membership to 250. In short order, Long Lane became one of Boston's largest and most vibrant congregations. Moorhead had a successful, 40-year-long ministry. The established Puritan churches referred to his congregation as the "Church of Presbyterian Strangers."

After Moorhead's death in 1773,[67] Long Lane was wracked by internal strife and went into sudden decline. The problems were a combination of ecclesiastical differences and political schism. Some parishioners favored the Presbyterian form of governance, while others supported the Congregational system. In the growing dispute with Great Britain, some cast their allegiance with the Crown while others assumed the "patriot" position. More controversy developed when John Murray, a youthful ministerial candidate who was an advocate for the then radical doctrine of universal salvation, applied for the position. He was not called.

65. Proprietors' Committee to Belknap, Boston, Jan. 30, 1787, *ibid.*, 6th ser., 4:326.

66. On the history of Long Lane Church, see Harriet E. Johnson, "The Early History of Arlington Street Church," *Proceedings of the Unitarian Historical Society*, Part II, 5 (1937): 15-33.

67. The broadside, "An Elegy to Miss Mary Moorhead, on the death of her father, the Rev. John Moorhead," by the acclaimed black poet Phillis Wheatley, was published in Boston in 1773.

During the Revolution, the church became moribund. For several years, its large, impressive meeting hall remained closed. In 1783, a decade after Moorhead's death and with the war at an end, the church was revived. The Presbyterian element managed to secure the appointment of one of its own, the Reverend Robert Annan of New York, as the congregation's spiritual head. But the internecine struggle persisted. A "defeated apostle," Annan left the church, and Boston, in 1786, whereupon the parishioners voted "that the Church and congregation do embrace the Congregational mode of government."

With a membership of a mere 30 families, Long Lane did not have the institutional stability or social prestige of the well-established Brattle Street or Old South societies in 1787, but it was a parish with possibilities. For someone in Belknap's position, the Church was a lifeline of opportunity. He could foresee nothing better, so he accepted its offer.[68] He participated in two installation meetings. At the second, held in the home of one of the church's deacons, a delegate read the letter of Belknap's dismissal from the Dover parish. The document publicly certified that Belknap had relinquished his pulpit with regret and was being sent to his new parish with "devout and enthusiastic commendations." The Long Lane Church fathers pledged Belknap a salary of 125 pounds, and promised more if the congregation grew and prospered.

For Belknap, aside from the favorable financial consideration, the most positive aspect of his new assignment was the location of the church. He was elated to be back in Boston. At almost the same moment he accepted the Long Lane job, Belknap received an offer for an editorial position from Mathew Carey, the progressive Philadelphia magazine publisher.[69] This post paid almost as much as the

68. Just before Belknap was installed, an anonymous parishioner of Long Lane, using the pseudonym "Moorhead's Ghost," sent a letter to a deacon of the church in which he questioned the minister-elect's orthodoxy. The critic accused Belknap of being a Universalist and follower of John Murray, no light indictment in those days. Belknap successfully defended himself and was installed on Apr. 4, 1787. Some key documents on this issue are printed in Marcou, *Belknap*, 142-146.

69. Hazard made the arrangements for the offer. See Carey to Hazard, Philadelphia, Jan. 11, 1787, Mass. Hist. Soc., *Coll.*, 6th ser., 4:324-325; Hazard to Belknap, New York, Jan. 20, 1787, *ibid.*, 5th ser., 2:449-453; Belknap to Hazard,

Long Lane position, but Belknap, while tempted, turned it down. As he explained to Hazard: "My fondness for Philadelphia is indeed great; but nothing, my dear sir, can exceed my attachment to this place [Boston]. Here are my natural, original friends, whom I have loved from my infancy; here are Mrs. Belknap's friends; here are the companions of my childhood and youth."[70] The Boston assignment also offered the promise of a liberal amount of free time to pursue his historical and literary interests. He no longer yearned for "a quiet and comfortable country life." The place of his birth and childhood beckoned him.

An ebullient Belknap left Dover and its dreary associations (and, no doubt, a joyous First Church) and took up residence in Boston in February 1787, the year in which the federal constitution was formulated. With his return, he laid the foundation of a new life. His final 11 years were happy and productive. He enjoyed a successful and serene ministry at the Long Lane Church. Unlike his experience in Dover, he was rewarded with periodic increases in salary.[71] He also supplemented his salary through his writings for periodicals and by tutoring students. No longer plagued with financial problems and with a lessening of domestic responsibilities, he became an active

Boston, Feb. 2, 1787, *ibid.*, 453-457; Hazard to Belknap, New York, Feb. 3, 1787, *ibid.*, 459-460. On Carey, the Irish immigrant who established his publishing business in Philadelphia in 1785 and subsequently became "the greatest publisher in America in the first two decades of the 19th century," see James N. Green, *Mathew Carey, Publisher and Patriot* (Philadelphia, 1985); and Earl L. Bradsher, *Mathew Carey, Editor, Author and Publisher: A Study in American Literary Development* (New York, 1912).

70. Belknap to Hazard, Boston, Feb. 2, 1787, Mass. Hist. Soc., *Coll.*, 5th ser., 2:454-455; Long Lane Church Records, Massachusetts Historical Society, 113-122. In his letter of acceptance, Belknap wrote: "From the Character which you bear among your Neighbours as well as you[r] own Promise expressed in your Votes, I have full reliance on you[r] sincere Intention to afford me, that 'comfortable support' which will keep my mind free from embarressment, with regard to externals and enable me to persue my Studies and attend to the several parts of my ministerial work with Cheerfulness." See 119-122.

71. Transactions of the . . . Church in Long Lane, Federal Street Church Records, 115, 133. The New England Historic Genealogical Society, Boston, owns a Belknap notebook which contains considerable information on the church during his tenure (deaths in the congregation, 1787-1796; members in 1793; communicants from 1787-1796; votes of the church, 1787; order of the communion service; an address by Belknap in 1794 on the communion service). I am indebted to Edward W. Hanson, who informed me of this document.

participant in the vibrant social, civic, educational, and cultural life of the city. He was no longer an intellectual recluse. He became a productive writer[72] and engaged in a wide spectrum of non-church activities, from serving on the Harvard Board of Overseers to founding an historical society. In 1792, Harvard awarded him an honorary doctorate.[73] He was one of Boston's brightest lights, "an enlivening and enlarging influence."[74]

72. Because Belknap contributed numerous essays to magazines and newspapers under pseudonyms, the full extent of his literary output is not known. Belknap also began to receive modest royalties from a hymnbook he published in 1797, *Sacred Poetry*. He intended the book for the use of his Long Lane congregation, but because it filled a general need many other New England churches purchased copies. According to Clifford Shipton, *Sacred Poetry* was for "forty years the most popular hymnal in New England." It went through numerous editions after Belknap's death. See *Sibley's Harvard Graduates*, 7: 487-488. For a negative appraisal of Belknap's hymnal, see Thomas Dawes, Jr., to Noah Webster, Boston, Mar. 27, 1823, in Emily Ellsworth Fowler Ford, ed., and Emily Ellsworth Ford Skeel, comp., *Notes on the Life of Noah Webster*, 2 vols. (New York, 1912), 2: 190-191.

73. Belknap informed Hazard that he was not particularly pleased with this honor. He had not sought the degree and would have "objected" to it and "suppressed it in embryo" but learned that some of his "best friends" had inspired it, and so he found himself obliged to "consent to the sacrifice." He added: "Perhaps you have the same idea of a doctorate that you have of a pumpkin,—that its belly is full of seed, which may, if properly managed, yield a large crop? If so, you must wait another season before I shall be prepared to give you an answer; for all depends upon *cultivation*. To be, as Pope says, 'stuck o'er with titles,' is what I never coveted. I have an ambition only to be useful in the world, and the thing which I most dread is to live so long as to be past doing any good." Belknap to Hazard, Boston, Aug. 27, 1792, Mass. Hist. Soc., *Coll.*, 5th ser., 3: 306-307. Samuel Adams, Francis Dana, Alexander Hamilton, John Hancock, John Lowell, Abiel Holmes, and Ebenezer Gay also received honorary degrees in 1792.

74. Eliot, "Jeremy Belknap," Mass. Hist. Soc., *Procs.*, 66 (1942): 98.

The Historian

He who rescues from oblivion interesting historical facts is beneficial to posterity as well as to his contemporaries; and the prospect
thereof to a benevolent mind causes that employment to be agreeable
and pleasant, which otherwise would be irksome and painful.

Thomas Hutchinson[1]

The longer I reflect on the nature of historical composition, the more
I am convinced that this scrupulous accuracy is necessary. The historian who records the events of his own time, is credited in proportion
to the opinion which the Public entertains with respect to his means of
information and his veracity. He who delineates the transactions of a
remote period, has no title to claim assent, unless he produces evidence in proof of his assertions. Without this, he may write an amusing
tale, but cannot be said to have composed an authentic history.

William Robertson[2]

O N August 3, 1788, a Sunday, Jeremy Belknap was invited to
the "Roxbury old church" to sermonize and conduct services.
"In the interval of service," a time when visiting preachers either
socialized with the host minister and his family and parishioners or
worked on sermon notes for the afternoon program, Belknap se-
cluded himself with the "ancient church records" of the Roxbury
parish. Upon his return home that evening he wrote Ebenezer Hazard: "some things there are very curious, and some which corrobo-
rate an idea which I have long had, and which I have heard you express, concerning the treatment which captive Indians met with from
our otherwise good forefathers. Old father [John] Eliot appears as an
honest man, and expresses a parental affection for the unhappy Indians, and would have saved the life of one in particular, if he could;
but the then Governour was inexorable. *Humanum est errare!*"[3]

Belknap's experience at Roxbury illustrates the powerful hold that

1. Thomas Hutchinson, *A Collection of Original Papers Relative to the History of the Colony of Massachusetts Bay* (Boston, 1769), 4: preface, I.

2. William Robertson, *The History of America*, 6th ed. (London, 1792), 1:
preface, xiv-xv.

3. Belknap to Hazard, Boston, Aug. 3, 1788, Mass. Hist. Soc., *Coll.*, 5th ser.,
3:56.

history had over him. History, not theology, was his consuming interest. He would fulfill his obligations as a minister, but when an opportunity for historical research presented itself he seized it. In his letter to Hazard, Belknap made no reference to his sermons or any other religious aspect of his day-long stay at the Roxbury church. He focused only on one subject, the "ancient church records."

Belknap's intellectual odyssey as an historian began in earnest during his dark days in Dover. Two activities sustained him during this trying period. One was his correspondence. He wrote regularly to friends in Boston who were men of learning, and he initiated and maintained contacts with savants in other parts of the nation and western Europe. These letters became his dram and drug. By exchanging ideas and publications with these serious-minded men, he kept up in a variety of fields that interested him, from astronomy to natural history. His correspondence connected him with a more impassioned life, with the world at large.

An even greater stimulus to his morale was his historical work. This, above all, made life bearable during years of frustration. Researching was a solace. Alone in his study, buried in his books and manuscripts, he could escape from the problems which made his life in provincial Dover a somber experience.

Soon after settling in Dover, Belknap became interested in the history of both the town and the state of New Hampshire. When he could break away from ministerial duties and other pressing obligations, he sought "to learn what I can from printed books and manuscripts, and the information of aged and intelligent persons, of the former state and affairs of this town and province."[4] From time to time, he traveled to remote sections of the state, seeking out docu-

4. Quoted in Jane B. Marcou, *The Life of Jeremy Belknap, D.D.: The Historian of New Hampshire, With Selections From His Correspondence and Other Writings* (New York, 1847), 47. It is interesting to note that Belknap requested his friends not to publicize his historical project. When soliciting information from strangers, he did not reveal that *he* was the author of the projected work. See Belknap to Rev. John Usher (of Bristol, R.I.), Mar. 30, 1773; Belknap to David Sewall (of York), Mar. 25, 1774. Letterbook, Belknap Papers, Massachusetts Historical Society. What was the reason for his secrecy? The only plausible explanation is that he was apprehensive of criticism by his parishioners and church fathers for not devoting every waking minute to his ministerial duties. It was not common for 18th-century ministers to engage in time-consuming, extracurricular activities.

ments and information. He "repeatedly searched" public offices for relevant sources. He consulted original surveys and spoke with "many persons who have been employed in surveying, masting, hunting and scouting; as well as in husbandry, manufactures, merchandise, navigation and fishery." To make certain "no source of information might be left unexplored," he composed and mailed out a printed "circular," or questionnaire, to the "several Clergymen, and other gentlemen of public character" in all sections of the state. While not all recipients of the circular responded, he did manage to accumulate a substantial body of information.[5]

"Hystoriography" became Belknap's "principal amusement," his "only pleasure."[6] As he wrote (in the third person in the preface of his *History of New Hampshire*): "Having met with some valuable manuscripts which were but little known, he began to extract and methodize the principal things in them; and this employment was (to speak in the style of a celebrated modern author) 'his hobby horse.'"[7]

Belknap's involvement in this project was not unusual for him. His interest in history was deeply rooted. While a boy in Boston he displayed an "inquisitive disposition in historical matters" and a "natural curiosity to enquire into the original settlement, progress, and improvement of the country which gave him birth."[8]

Who, or what influences, inspired his interest? One factor was the religious and cultural crucible in which he was molded. The study of human history was a *sine qua non* of the Puritans. They were driven by a sense of history. They viewed their migration to Massachusetts, the "errand into the wilderness," as part of God's master plan for mankind. Their mission had a key role in the drama of Christian eschatology. They believed that all of human history led up to their exodus from England, that their settlement in Massachusetts lay at the heart of the design of Providence. They therefore regarded themselves as main actors in one of the most momentous episodes of

5. Jeremy Belknap, *The History of New Hampshire*, 3 vols. (Philadelphia and Boston, 1784-1792), 3: preface, iii.

6. John Eliot to Belknap, July 31, 1781, Mass. Hist. Soc., *Coll.*, 6th ser., 4: 213; Marcou, *Belknap*, 47.

7. *History of New Hampshire*, 1: preface, vii.

8. *Ibid.*, iii.

world history.[9] They were a "peculiar people." This was the essence of the Puritan notion of American exceptionalism.

Puritan children were made aware of the clan's unique historical mission either by parents, their ministers, or both. Because of this intense conditioning, many developed a heightened historical consciousness. Certainly Belknap did.

A second likely cause of Belknap's pronounced historical bent was the powerful nationalistic surge that swept across the United States after the successful conclusion of the American Revolution. Belknap was an ardent nationalist; Charles Cole has called him a "pioneer nationalist."[10] Belknap's love for his native land was a natural extension of his patriotism during the American Revolution.

Not that he spontaneously bloomed as a full-blown rebel in the manner of a Sam Adams or James Otis. Belknap evolved into a patriot. When the political crisis with Great Britain first developed in the late 1760s and early 1770s, he assumed a moderate, watch-and-wait position.[11] Psychologically and philosophically, he was not given to violence or an irrevocable break with the mother country.

As the breach widened, he moved steadily in the direction of the Whig cause and became a "warm friend of the revolution."[12] When the British Parliament passed the four punitive acts against Massachusetts in reaction to the Boston Tea Party Belknap became a rabid rebel and a leading member of the "black regiment," as the Loyalists called the ministers who supported the Revolution. From that time on, he lambasted the British from the pulpit and with his pen.[13] After

9. This subject is treated in depth in Perry Miller's two classic studies of Puritanism: *The New England Mind: From Colony to Province* (Cambridge, Mass., 1953); and *The New England Mind: The Seventeenth Century* (New York, 1939). See also Kenneth Murdock, *Literature and Theology in Colonial New England* (Cambridge, Mass., 1949).

10. "Jeremy Belknap: Pioneer Nationalist," *New England Quarterly*, 10: 743-751 (1937).

11. George Kirsch tracks Belknap's metamorphosis from a moderate Whig to a confirmed patriot in "Jeremy Belknap and the Coming of the Revolution," *Historical New Hampshire*, 29 (1974): 151-172.

12. John Thornton Kirkland, *A Sermon Delivered at Interment of Jeremy Belknap, D.D.* (Boston, 1798), 15.

13. Because of Belknap's forceful and outspoken opposition to British policy, the New Hampshire Committee of Safety asked him to serve as the resident

the war, Belknap shared the spirit of exaltation his victorious countrymen felt. He, too, gloried in being an American.

While Belknap's love of country encompassed most of the major aspects of early American nationalism, from the belief in a strong central government to the desirability of unified economic development and self-sufficiency, it was tinged with a pronounced cultural hue.[14] His vision of America was of a nation bursting with activities in the arts, sciences, and humanities. Three years before the Revolution ended, he proposed a "Congress of Philosophers as well as of Statesmen." He added: "I am so far an enthusiast in the cause of America as to wish she may shine Mistress of the Sciences, as well as the Asylum of Liberty."[15] "I believe this is the historical Age," David Hume asserted in 1770," and this [Scotland] the historical Nation."[16] For Belknap, the "historical Age" began with the completion of the American Revolution and the founding of the United States, and the "historical Nation" was his own native land.

Belknap hoped to make his contribution to the development of an American Elysium through his writings. All of his historical works dealt with American themes. He was one of a growing legion of cultural nationalists who were becoming stridently self-confident

chaplain of the 1,200-man force that rushed to the assistance of their beleaguered Massachusetts brethren in April 1775. Belknap was forced to decline the assignment because of ill health and familial considerations. He did travel to Cambridge and preach to the citizen-soldiers while they participated in the siege of Boston. Belknap's contributions as a patriot during the Revolution are recounted in George B. Spaulding, *The Dover Pulpit During the Revolutionary War . . .* (Dover, 1876).

14. See Cole, "Belknap, Pioneer Nationalist," 743-751.

15. Belknap to Hazard, Feb. 4, 1780, Mass. Hist. Soc., *Coll.*, 5th ser., 2:255. Belknap gave full expression to his nationalistic spirit in a letter to Sen. Paine Wingate in 1789: "The body to which you belong is truly respectable and its transactions must be very important—not only to the present but the future generations. This idea so strongly impresses my mind that I feel a kind of veneration for every one of its productions, as being the deliberative wisdom of this whole Continent which is every day rising into vigor and manhood and taking rank among the most celebrated republicks of the world. I feel a kind of national pride in being a member of this republick and in the thought that such great and worthy characters as Washington, Adams etc. etc. are *my* fellow citizens." Belknap to Wingate, Boston, July 18, 1789, Historical Society of Pennsylvania.

16. Hume to William Strahan, Aug., 1770, *The Letters of David Hume*, ed. J. Y. T. Greig, 2 vols. (Oxford, 1932), 2:230.

Americans and producing books reflective of their feelings. Prime examples were Noah Webster's *American Spelling Book* (1783), Nicholas Pike's *American Arithmetic* (1788), and Jedidiah Morse's *American Geography* (1789).

Family influences also had a hand in developing Belknap's love of history. On his mother's side, the blood of the illustrious Mather family flowed through his veins, and there was no more historically minded family in New England than the Mathers. Richard, Increase, and Cotton Mather were the apotheosis of New England history.[17] Like Winston Churchill, Belknap absorbed history "through the skin."

Also, through the mind. The chief transmitter was the Reverend Thomas Prince, one of Puritanism's most industrious historians and an "American pioneer in scientific historical writing."[18] Prince baptized Belknap and, as the boy matured, became not only his spiritual mentor but his intellectual preceptor as well. Whereas great-uncle Mather Byles stimulated Belknap's literary appetite, the learned Prince sharpened his historical sensibilities, provided him with a value structure, and served as a proper role model.

As an historian, Prince stood apart from his contemporaries. His insatiable interest in local and regional history was not unique, but his pertinacity as a researcher did remove him from the realm of the ordinary. According to Clifford Shipton, "it was commonly said that when he set himself down to work in a library he lost all sense of time and remained until his host dug him out to feed him or to send him home to Mrs. Prince."[19]

What particularly seized Prince's attention and kept him engrossed were original sources. He was fascinated by documents. He used them because of his passion for factual accuracy. As he wrote in the preface of his *Chronological History of New England*: "It is *Exactness* I aim at, and would not have the least Mistake if possible

17. See Robert Middlekauff, *The Mathers: Three Generations of Puritan Intellectuals, 1596-1728* (New York, 1971).

18. For an analysis of Prince as an historian, see Michael Kraus, *The Writing of American History* (Norman, Okla., 1953), 47-49. Prince's interest in history developed at an early age. He was strongly influenced by Cotton Mather.

19. Shipton, *Sibley's Harvard Graduates*, 5:349.

pass to the World."[20] He was convinced that there was a direct link between primary sources and historical truth.

Prince was also a voracious collector of historical materials bearing upon New England. The collecting "disease" afflicted him as a youngster. When he entered Harvard in 1703 (at age 16), he intensified his search for rare books and manuscripts. During his long ministerial career, he constantly solicited primary materials from fellow clergymen in New England. He also requested basic information on the histories of their respective communities.

Prince's standard technique was to circulate a detailed, printed questionnaire to these "learned gentlemen." It was framed as a form letter. Prince asked about the history and organization of their towns and sought information on their churches, schools, "Teaching or Ruling Elders," birth and death statistics, and *"the remarkable Providences* that have befallen your Town or the People in it, from the Beginning to the present Time, as Earthquakes, Tempests, Inundations, extraordinary Floods, Droughts, Fires, Epidemical Sicknesses, awful Deaths, or any other strange Occurrences, as far as can be recollected." Prince concluded with the admonition that his correspondents "be as *Precise* as possible in the *Dates,* both as to *Year, Month* and *Day,* of all your Articles, as well as *Certain* in the *Facts* related; that so the Publick may depend on the Truth and Accuracy of these Collections."[21]

Over a period of 50 years, Prince amassed one of the largest private libraries in the American colonies. It consisted of over 2,000 books, assorted manuscripts, pamphlets, maps, and other primary sources. This was his celebrated "New England Library" which, according to Edmund S. Morgan, was "one of the greatest collections of its kind" in America.[22] For an historian, it was a veritable treasure trove.

20. Thomas Prince, *A Chronological History of New England In the Form of Annals* . . . , 2 vols. (Boston, 1736-1755), 1: preface, ix.

21. One of these questionnaires, dated Feb. 20, 1728/29 (Boston, 1728/29) is attached to a copy of Prince's *Chronological History* in the Massachusetts Historical Society.

22. Edmund Sears Morgan, *The Puritan Family: Essays on Religion and Domestic Relations in Seventeenth-Century New England* (Boston, 1944), foreword. On the contents of the collection, see *The Prince Library: A Catalogue of the Collection of Books and Manuscripts Which Formerly Belonged to the Reverend*

Prince intended to use these materials in his projected "Chronological History of New England." Because he began with the Creation and never carried the study beyond the post-settlement period, he made only limited use of his collection. While Prince's study was —and still is—regarded as one of the better historical works produced by a colonial American, it is marred by flaws which limit its usefulness. Characterized by a spiritless style, it is aridly factual and lacks interpretation. Prince enjoyed an intercolonial reputation as one of the leading scholars in America, but he was not an accomplished historian. As Clifford Shipton has written: "He was indeed a far better historian than the Mathers, Hubbard or Niles, but only in promise, not achievement."[23]

Prince was the major influence in the historical conditioning of Belknap, helping to shape his convictions, thought, and outlook. Belknap acknowledged that he was "educated" under Prince "whose memory he [Belknap] shall always revere."[24]

There is a striking similarity between Belknap and Prince as historians. Like Prince, Belknap specialized in New England history, was a tireless researcher, displayed an uncommon zeal for factual accuracy, and used original sources whenever possible. Moreover, Belknap collected historical materials and data with an

Thomas Prince, and was by him Bequeathed to the Old South Church, and is now Deposited in the Public Library of the City of Boston (Boston, 1870), introduction by Justin Winsor. The significance of Prince's library was underscored by John Adams's action when the Massachusetts General Court, in 1774, appointed him to defend the Commonwealth's northern and western territorial claims. Adams did not go to the provincial secretary's office or the Harvard College library to research the issue. Rather, he went "to the Balcony of Dr. Sewalls Church [Old South], where Mr. Prince had deposited the amplest Collection of Books, Pamphlets, Records and Manuscripts relative to this Country which I ever saw, and which as I presume ever was made." Autobiography of John Adams, Fall, 1773, Adams Papers, Massachusetts Historical Society. Many materials from Prince's library were lost during the Revolution. The patriots blamed the "British Barbarians" who had used the Church as a riding school. Clifford Shipton and other modern scholars have asserted that Bostonians were equally to blame for the losses sustained by the library. Some of them borrowed materials and failed to return them. No one was in charge of the collection. The remains of Prince's collection are now housed in the Boston Public Library.

23. Shipton, *Sibley's Harvard Graduates*, 5:355.
24. Belknap, *History of New Hampshire*, 1: preface, vii.

intensity that might well have astounded even the acquisitive Prince.

It was not merely coincidence that Belknap, in his most significant historical writing, *The History of New Hampshire,* paid special tribute to the "late accurate and indefatigable Mr. PRINCE of Boston."[25] His choice of adjectives is particularly revealing since it provides insight into his own values as an historian. For Prince, as for Belknap, accuracy and thorough research were the historian's prime *desiderata.*[26]

In only one particular did Belknap deviate sharply from his mentor. Belknap had a much more liberal attitude than Prince toward the use of historical materials. In his will, Prince decreed that his remarkable collection should be kept intact and "no person shall borrow any book or paper therefrom." Belknap always opposed such a restrictive policy. He believed in the open use of these materials.[27] Just as ideas should not be circumscribed, so, too, books and documents must circulate and be made accessible to researchers.

Harvard College also played a role in stimulating Belknap's interest in history. While a student in Cambridge, he read extensively in the works of ancient and modern European history. One of his favorite authors was the 17th-century Englishman Laurence Echard, who wrote some key works on Roman history. Belknap copied one of Echard's statements into his commonplace book, which he called "Quotidiana Miscellanea": "there are required so many Qualifications and Accomplishments in an *Historian,* and so much care and niceness in writing an History, that some have reckon'd it *One of the Most Difficult Labours Human Nature is capable of.*"[28] The words were Echard's, but the emphasis was Belknap's.

25. *Ibid.*

26. *Ibid.,* viii. After reading a portion of George Chalmers's *Political Annals of the Present United Colonies* (London, 1780), Belknap informed John Adams that Chalmers had "the spirit of indefatigable enquiry which is necessary in a historian." Belknap to Adams, July 18, 1789, Adams Papers, Massachusetts Historical Society.

27. Marcou, *Belknap,* 187.

28. Belknap Papers, Massachusetts Historical Society. Echard's work also impressed another historian who was a contemporary—Edward Gibbon. Gibbon's "first introduction to the historic scenes" was the *Continuation of Echard's Roman History.* He read it in 1751 at age 14 and called it an "intellectual feast." See *Gibbon's Autobiography,* ed. M. M. Reese (London, 1971), 25-26.

In the last three decades of his life, Belknap mounted his "hobby horse" at every available opportunity. He contributed innumerable essays and historical ephemera to magazines and newspapers.[29] He also became involved in two major publishing projects.

One was his *History of New Hampshire*. He worked on this study, by fits and starts, for almost 22 years. It eventually developed into three volumes. He published the first volume in 1784, the second in 1791, and the third in 1792.[30] The *History* was Belknap's principal intellectual achievement, and his reputation as an historian rests chiefly on this work. It placed him among the first rank of his generation of American historians.

In form and content, there is a striking difference between the first two volumes and the third. The first two consist largely of political, legal, and military history and follow a chronological path, beginning with the period of European exploration in North America in the 15th century (the voyages of John Smith and John Mason) and extending to the formulation and ratification of the federal constitution in the 1780s. In every way, it was the conventional format for that era.

The third volume stands out as an independent segment of the trilogy. Its contents are an historical potpourri and bear a striking resemblance to Thomas Jefferson's *Notes on the State of Virginia*, published in 1785. Belknap discussed subjects topically: geography, climate, Indian monuments and relics, commerce, transportation, education, religion, industry, population, literature—and many more. He gave a strong emphasis to natural history, one of his personal interests.

The most conspicuous feature of volume three is its plethora of

29. Because of Belknap's many contributions to the *Columbian Magazine*, *American Museum*, *American Magazine*, and *Massachusetts Magazine*, Kenneth Silverman has written: "he became probably the first free-lance magazine writer in America, sought by competing editors who wished to publish parts of his large collection of literary and historical documents." *A Cultural History of the American Revolution* (New York, 1976), 489.

30. Each volume of the first edition was produced by a different printer. Robert Aitken of Philadelphia printed volume I; Isaiah Thomas and Alexander Young of Boston printed volume II; and Joseph Belknap (Jeremy's son) and Alexander Young of Boston printed volume III.

factual data and statistics. It is very much like a modern encyclopedia. In adopting this format, Belknap revealed the influence of contemporary trends. As Patricia Cline Cohen has shown in her suggestive study, *A Calculating People: The Spread of Numeracy in Early America*,[31] following the Revolution, American men of letters emulated their European peers and incorporated "authentic facts" and "statisticks" into their historical and geographical writings. Why? Because these "men of the new republic" were convinced that truth lay on a bedrock of factual and numerical data. Nationalists to the core, these authors were seeking to validate the "great experiment in republicanism" and define the true nature of American society. They firmly believed that they could achieve these objectives by setting forth the "authentic facts" and qualifying "statisticks." In this way they could portend trends and detect social change. As Cohen has written: "Implicit in the new style was an assumption of historical progress: the facts of today were important to know because they presaged the improvements of tomorrow."[32]

Belknap's *History of New Hampshire* has had a curious history of its own. Because it lacked a grand theme, was devoid of dramatic doings and Olympian personalities, was narrow in geographic scope, and dealt with an area that had only a marginal importance in the history of colonial America, it did not become a literary sensation or attract a vast admiring public upon its first appearance. Notwithstanding Belknap's aggressive, personal, promotional efforts, there were few purchasers. Wide time gaps between the publication of the three volumes also hurt sales. The interest of book buyers could not be sustained by piecemeal history.

Nor did the study make a powerful impact upon contemporary literati. Those authors who specialized in historical writings, such as David Ramsay of South Carolina, praised it highly,[33] but there were

31. (Chicago and London, 1985).

32. Cohen, *Calculating People*, see ch. 5.

33. Ramsay wrote to Belknap on Aug. 11, 1792: "If all the existing records either in print or manuscript which respect the first settlement of Carolina were collected together in hands of ingenious men who would devote their time to elucidate our early history it would be impossible for them to give such a particular and interesting narrative as you have done in your three volumes containing the history of New Hampshire . . . I wish such men could be found

few of these in the nation. During the 19th century, the work continued to remain relatively unknown, although periodically a prominent
man of letters, like William Cullen Bryant and Alexis de Tocqueville, wrote of it with high appreciation.[34]

The standing of the *History* has risen sharply in the 20th century.
A number of reputable scholars have acclaimed it as a classic American regional history. Belknap's stature as an historian has correspondingly grown. He, too, has been showered with accolades. A
few commentators have ranked him with such Promethean figures
of American historical literature as George Bancroft, Francis Parkman, and Henry Adams.[35]

What are the special features of the *History* which have earned
for it such glowing assessments? Modern critics have stressed three
major strengths. First and foremost, they lavish praise upon Belknap's erudition. His work is based upon careful, exhaustive research and its scholarship is impeccably accurate. Secondly, they
give him high marks as a stylist; one commentator refers to him as

who would take equal pains in writing the history of each state." In Correspondence of the Corresponding Secretary, 1791-1798, Massachusetts Historical Society. The publication also was praised by the German scholar, Christoph Daniel (or C. D.) Ebeling, who became one of Belknap's correspondents:
"Your excellent History of New Hampshire meets with the due applause in
Germany, where I introduced several copies. In the Göttingen Review . . . it has
been reviewed with great applause, as well on account of the materials as the
true elegance of historical stile." Ebeling to Belknap, Hamburg, Sept. 20, 1794,
Mass. Hist. Soc., *Coll.*, 6th ser., 4:581. On Oct. 1, 1796, Ebeling suggested to
Belknap that he should write a history of Massachusetts: "That would be a
valuable present to the world." *Ibid.*, 607.

34. See Eliot, "Jeremy Belknap," Mass. Hist. Soc., *Procs.*, 66 (1944): 102-103;
Tocqueville, *Democracy in America*, 2 vols. (New York, 1961), 2:367.

35. See G. T. Lord, ed., *Belknap's New Hampshire, An Account of the State
in 1792*, facsimile edition of vol. 3 of *The History of New Hampshire* (Hampton, 1973), preface, v; Kraus, *Writing of American History*, 73, 76; John Spen-
cer Bassett, *The Middle Group of American Historians* (New York, 1917), 41-
43; Shipton, *Sibley's Harvard Graduates*, 15:180. The *Cambridge History of
American Literature*, ed. William P. Trent, John Erskine, Stuart P. Sherman, and
Carl Van Doren, 3 vols. (New York, 1947), 2:106, rendered this judgment on
Belknap's *History*: "Of the state histories that appeared in this period a few are
worthy of mention. Jeremy Belknap (1744-1798) wrote a *History of New Hampshire* (three volumes, 1784-92) which is of the first rank in our historical com-
positions. Had its theme been more extended, it would have become a household
memory in the country."

the "belletristic parson" and describes him as a "conscious craftsman in historical letters."[36]

A third chief feature of the *History* is its distinctly modernist character. It is not a conventional 18th-century history. Whereas earlier New England historians and most, if not all, of Belknap's contemporaries wrote from predisposed points of view, he based his conclusions upon primary evidence after an exhaustive, critical analysis. In short, he strove to write "objective" history.

Further, he placed an inordinate stress on the "rational and active powers" of people and, correspondingly, discounted the influence of the supernatural (including Divine Providence) in the affairs of humankind. While Belknap did not entirely remove God from the historical stage, he placed Him far from the main flow of human action. God was not the dominant force in Belknap's exposition. The minister wrote almost purely secular history. He did not offer religious answers to questions about historical causation. He posited reason as the determinate force in history and rejected omens, portents, superstition, and miracles.[37] In this sense, he was an anomaly for his age. He was at the forefront of the movement to liberate the writing of history from its subservience to theology and spectral evidence.

Modern critics have also praised Belknap's uncommonly liberal and tolerant attitude toward Native Americans and Black slaves. He severely criticized his Puritan forefathers and his contemporaries for their insensitive, inhumane treatment of these two groups.[38]

36. Sidney Kaplan, "The History of New Hampshire: Jeremy Belknap as Literary Craftsman," *William and Mary Quarterly*, 3rd ser., 21 (1964): 19-20. This is a perceptive appraisal of the literary qualities of the *History*.

37. These aspects of the *History* are analyzed in Jere Daniell, "Jeremy Belknap and the History of New Hampshire," in *The Colonial Legacy*, ed. Lawrence H. Leder (New York, 1973), 4:241-264. In 1789, Belknap borrowed Cotton Mather's *Wonders of the Invisible World* from the Harvard College Library. Mather's proclivity for the supernatural amused Belknap. He wrote Hazard, "I wish you was here to laugh with me" at Mather's study, and then he quoted some "choice" extracts in which the eminent Puritan had affirmed the powers of the "Devil" in human activity. Belknap regarded Mather as pedantic and credulous and an amusing curiosity. Belknap to Hazard, Boston, Oct. 22, 1789, Mass. Hist. Soc., *Coll.*, 5th ser., 3:198-199.

38. George Kirsch has examined this topic in "Jeremy Belknap and the Problem of Blacks and Indians in Early America," *Historical New Hampshire*, 34 (1979): 202-222.

Again, this was not the traditional attitude of the minister's period.

The use of primary sources, the critical examination of these materials, the striving for factual accuracy and objectivity, the rejection of the supernatural and divinity in historical causation, the stress on reason and human initiative in history—these were the principal elements in the development of the historical aspects of the social sciences in the 18th century. David Hume, Edward Gibbon, William Robertson, Voltaire, and Montesquieu, among the European philosophes, led the way in this movement. These historian-philosophers sought to make history the science of man.[39]

If he was not the first historian-social scientist in the United States, Belknap was certainly in the vanguard of this movement. Either consciously or unconsciously, he had absorbed the basic values of the philosophes, and his historical writings, particularly his study of New Hampshire, showed how profoundly he had been influenced by these new intellectual currents.

Belknap's study of New Hampshire, as well as Jefferson's book on Virginia, marked the beginning of a rash of local and regional histories following the Revolution as the nationalistic impulse grew stronger. In 1794, Samuel Williams came forth with *The Natural and Civil History of Vermont,* a work consciously modeled after Belknap's third volume. James Sullivan produced *The History of the District of Maine* in 1795. In 1797 and 1798, Robert Proud published a two-volume history of Pennsylvania. Ira Allen's *Natural and Civil History of the State of Vermont* and George Minot's *Continuation of the History of the Province of the Massachusetts Bay Colony* appeared in 1798.

Belknap's second major historical project was a multi-volume collection of biographical sketches of prominent personalities associated with American history, an 18th-century precursor of the *Dictionary of American Biography.* In 1779, Belknap had urged this project upon Ebenezer Hazard, who was already collecting documents on American history for a proposed publication of state papers. "In the course of your travels and researches into antiquity," wrote Belknap, "you will naturally become acquainted with the

39. See Peter Gay, *The Enlightenment: An Interpretation* (New York, 1969), 2:368-396.

characters of many persons whose memories deserve regard either as statesmen, scholars, patriots, soldiers, or otherwise. Might not a collection of these in the form of a biographical dictionary be an useful work?"[40]

Hazard was "charmed" by Belknap's proposal but did not wish to undertake it because he would be diverted from his main mission. He further informed Belknap that, concurrent with his major undertaking, he was forming "an American Geography." It was not possible for him to take on a third project. He urged Belknap to "go on with it."[41]

Belknap decided to tackle the assignment. He began collecting biographical data in desultory fashion, but he accelerated his collecting when in 1789 William Spotswood, editor of the *Columbian Magazine*, an ardently patriotic Philadelphia journal, requested some entries.[42] Spotswood was familiar with Belknap's literary talents, having recently published in serial form the minister's satirical allegory of the history of the colonies titled *The Foresters: An Historical Romance.*

Because the Philadelphia literary periodical had a strong reputation and wide circulation among the learned element along the Atlantic seaboard, and also because it paid a liberal fee to its contributors, Belknap agreed to provide the sketches. He produced three (John Winthrop, Ferdinando Gorges, and John Smith) between January and December 1788. They were published anonymously under the rubric: "The American Plutarch."[43] In succeeding years, Belknap

40. Belknap to Hazard, Dover, Feb. 2, 1779, Mass. Hist. Soc., *Coll.*, 5th ser., 2:2-3.

41. Hazard to Belknap, Philadelphia, Apr. 19, 1779, *ibid.*, 4-5. See also, Belknap to Hazard, Jamaica Plain, Aug. 4, 1779, *ibid.*, 7-8, *passim*. On Dec. 28, 1779, Belknap informed Hazard that John Eliot "seems inclined" to undertake the biographical project. He implored Hazard to "urge *it* on him." *Ibid.*, 26. Belknap's friends were constantly urging him to take on historical writing projects. On Jan. 5, 1791, Benjamin Rush of Philadelphia wrote Belknap as follows: "I wish very much to see a short and faithful history of the establishment of the federal government. . . . Suppose you undertake it." Mass. Hist. Soc., *Coll.*, 6th ser., 4:474.

42. For an account of the *Columbian Magazine*, see Lyon N. Richardson, *A History of Early American Magazines, 1741-1789* (New York, 1931), 278-299. Belknap's relationship with the journal is discussed on 279, 281-285.

43. Only a few of Belknap's close friends knew that he was the "American Plutarch." On Nov. 27, 1788, Hazard wrote Belknap: "N.W. [Noah Webster]

continued his research when time allowed and, in 1794, published his first volume of the *American Biography*.

The book was divided into three distinct sections. Belknap began with a "Preliminary Dissertation" on the exploration and circumnavigation of the African coast by the Phoenicians, Egyptians, Carthaginians, and other ancient adventurers. He then provided a detailed chronology of voyages to America by European explorers prior to the settlement of Plymouth in 1620. Next came the heart of the work, articles on the European explorers, from Biron (Bjorn) the Norseman, the supposed discoverer of Newfoundland, to the legendary Columbus, to the equally famous Henry Hudson. Belknap's list included every major adventurer and explorer and a number of minor ones, such as DeFuca, de Poutrincourt, and DeMonts.

A second volume was published in 1798, shortly after Belknap's death. Nearly the first quarter of this work dealt with the founding and settlement of Virginia by Thomas Smith, George Somers, and other English stalwarts. Next Belknap traced the exploits of the founders of New England, from Bartholomew Gosnold to the prominent Pilgrim and Puritan cohort: John Robinson, John Carver, William Bradford, William Brewster, Edward Winslow, both John Winthrops (elder and younger), and lesser figures. He concluded the volume with essays on George Calvert, the founder of Maryland, and William Penn, the developer of Pennsylvania.

Belknap actively collected information for a third volume, which was to treat historical personalities relating to the later period of New England,[44] but his death ended the project.[45] His notes for the

suspects, and, indeed, is 'pretty sure,' that you are the American Plutarch, because no man but yourself can possess sufficient materials for the purpose," Mass. Hist. Soc., *Coll.*, 5th ser., 3:77.

44. See, for example, Belknap to Jedidiah Morse, Boston, Mar. 10, 1798, Hist. Soc. of Pennsylvania, Dreer Collection, American Prose Writers; Belknap requested information on John Harvard: "give me a copy of *every thing* which can be found concerning him" and "any *Tradition* that may possibly have escaped the grasp of oblivion." See also, Belknap to the Reverend McClure, Boston, July 13, 1793, Hist. Soc. of Pennsylvania, Gratz Collection; Belknap requested information on a host of prominent Connecticut figures, as well as documents. His correspondent was from Windsor, Connecticut.

45. After Belknap's death, other authors sought to supplement his pioneer work as "biography mania" took hold. In 1809, John Eliot published a two-volume dictionary of American biography. Lacking in substance, it was regarded

uncompleted volume survive, a part of the Society's Belknap Papers.

Belknap's peers were impressed with his biographical study, which was an innovative work for that era. Modern critics have been less enthusiastic about the publication. They have credited Belknap with a craftsmanlike performance but regard the study as flawed. They have noted weaknesses in conception and structure and called attention to Belknap's heavy reliance upon published sources and secondary works.[46] In his defense, Belknap did not have access to primary sources except published documents. His study was vulnerable to the charge that it lacked originality. While it elevated his reputation as a productive man of letters among his contemporaries, it did not bring him enduring fame. Today, *American Biography* stands out as a literary museum piece.

There were only a handful of historians in the United States in the post-Revolution.[47] All were "amateurs"—that is, they did not derive their livelihoods from their historical writings. Belknap was among the most accomplished of these gentlemen-scholars. He also adhered to a value system that was not common for his era.

While an ardent reader of literary and scientific writings, Belknap regarded history as the most noble form of letters. He loved the subject passionately and sought to promote it at every turn. At the Harvard Commencement of 1787, for example, he was delighted to hear two young graduates give public testimony to the importance of history. In a highly patriotic address on "The Importance and

as a failure in learned circles. That same year, William Allen, later president of Dartmouth College, produced a creditable biographical dictionary, but it, too, failed to measure up to Belknap's factual style. The most successful of this genre was Jared Sparks's impressive 25-volume *Library of American Biography* series, which was published between 1834 and 1848.

46. For example, see George Kirsch, *Jeremy Belknap: A Biography* (New York, 1982), 131.

47. For a discussion of the historians and the state of historiography in this period, see Kraus, *Writing of American History*, ch. 4; Ralph N. Miller, "The Historians Discover America: A Study of American Historical Writing in the 18th Century" (Ph.D. diss., Northwestern Univ., 1946); Lawrence Buell, *New England Literary Culture: From Revolution Through Renaissance* (Cambridge, 1986), 195-196, 214-218, *passim*; Bassett, *Middle Group of American Historians*, 11-49; David D. van Tassel, *Recording America's Past: An Interpretation of the Development of Historical Studies in America, 1607-1884* (Chicago, 1960), 31-86.

Necessity of Publick Faith to the Well-being of a Community," John
Quincy Adams, 20 years old, stated: "The muses, disgusted with the
depravity both of taste and morals, which prevail in Europe, would
soon take up their abode in these blissful seats of liberty and peace;
here would they form historians, who should relate, and poets who
should sing the glories of our country."[48] These prophetic words
made a powerful impact upon Belknap. He was further pleased
when a second student, Thaddeus Mason Harris, presented an "English poem" in praise of history. Belknap sought the permission of
both scholars to have their offerings printed in the *Columbian Magazine*. Harris declined Belknap's request, but Adams accepted after
some delicate negotiating.[49]

In Belknap's scale of values, the search for historical truth took
precedence even over theological scholarship. Upon learning from a
correspondent that Charles Thomson, who had served as secretary
of the Continental Congress and been an eyewitness to some of the
most dramatic and significant events of American history, was writing a new translation of the Bible, Belknap caustically responded:
"How much better had *he* been employed in telling us some of the
secrets of the old Congress!!"[50]

Belknap regarded the writing of history as one of the most formi-
dable of intellectual challenges. Echard's statement, noted earlier,

48. Adams's address is printed in the *Columbian Magazine*, 1 (1787): 625-
628. Adams was responding to the crisis provoked by Shays's rebellion. Seeking
to "revive the drooping spirit," he appealed for a renewal of American patriotism. His reference to history came near the end of his address.

49. See Lawrence S. Mayo, "Jeremy Belknap and J. Q. Adams, 1787," Mass.
Hist. Soc., *Procs.*, 59 (1925-26): 203-209. When requesting Adams's permission,
Belknap wrote that he also planned to publish Harris's poem as a companion
piece. Adams acceded to Belknap's request but on the condition that the two
works appear jointly. Harris declined Belknap's offer. Belknap then wrote Adams imploring him to "take off the Embargo." Adams subsequently relented.
The Belknap-Adams correspondence is printed in the article cited above. The
implacable Harris later became librarian of Harvard, then minister of the First
Church in Dorchester.

50. Belknap to Hazard, Boston, Aug. 1, 1792, Belknap Papers, Massachusetts
Historical Society. Unknown to Belknap, Thomson did write a history of the
American Revolution, using sources he had gathered, but he burned the manuscript. He had been critical of some of the American revolutionaries and was
fearful of public reaction. See van Tassel, *Recording America's Past*, 34.

could have served as his creed. He never forgot these words. Twenty-five years after he first read them at Harvard, he was still citing them.[51]

Belknap bristled when anyone averred that writing history was a simple task. In a letter to Hazard in 1784, he took exception to the renowned Dr. Samuel Johnson, who had written in *The Rambler*, No. 122:

It is natural to believe . . . that no writer has a more easy task than the historian. The philosopher has the works of omniscience to examine; and is, therefore, engaged in disquisitions, to which finite intellects are utterly unequal. The poet trusts to his invention, and is not only in danger of those inconsistencies, to which every one is exposed by departure from truth; but may be censured as well for deficiencies of matter, as for irregularity of disposition, or impropriety of ornament. But the happy historian has no other labour than of gathering what tradition pours down before him, or records treasure for his use. He has only the actions and designs of men like himself to conceive and to relate; he is not to form, but copy characters, and, therefore, is not blamed for the inconsistency of statesmen, the injustice of tyrants, or the cowardice of commanders. The difficulty of making variety consistent, or uniting probability with surprise, needs not to disturb him; the manners and actions of his personages are already fixed; his materials are provided and put into his hands, and he is at leisure to employ all his powers in arranging and displaying them.[52]

"One may venture any bet," Belknap sarcastically noted, "that, at the time when this number of the Rambler was composed, Dr. J. had not undertaken an History."[53] In refuting Johnson, Belknap

51. Belknap to Hazard, Dover, Jan. 13, 1784, Mass. Hist. Soc., *Coll.*, 5th ser., 2:295.

52. Johnson's essay was dated May 21, 1751, 81-82. James Boswell records a similar point of view: "He [Johnson] said that great parts were not requisite for a historian, as in that kind of composition all the greatest powers of the human mind are quiescent. 'He has facts ready to his hand, so he has no exercise of invention. Imagination is not required in any high degree; only about as much as is used in the lower parts of poetry. Some penetration, accuracy, and colouring will fit a man for such a task, who can give the application which is necessary,'" *Boswell's London Journal, 1762-1763*, ed. Frederick A. Pottle (New York, 1950), 293.

53. Belknap to Hazard, Jan. 13, 1784, Mass. Hist. Soc., *Coll.*, 5th ser., 2:294. In addition to Belknap, many others have charged Johnson with being insensi-

underscored the prodigious problems a "happy historian" of New England faced as he practiced his craft:

But if he [Johnson] had to write the History of a country, and to search for his materials wheresoever they were likely or *not likely* to be found; if he was to find that the 'treasures' contained in 'records' are to be explained by private papers, and that these are to be sought in the garrets and rat-holes of old houses, when not one in a hundred that he was obliged to handle and decipher would repay him for the trouble; that 'tradition,' whatever it might 'pour down,' is always to be suspected and examined; and that the means of examination are not always to be obtained,—in short, if he had to go through the drudgery which you and I are pretty tolerably acquainted with, and to humour the passions of those we are obliged to, all the while, he would be fully sensible that to write an History as it should be is not so easy a work.[54]

To another correspondent in early 1785, Belknap conveyed similar sentiments: "None but those who have tried it can tell what is the trouble of writing an history out of fresh materials as I have. Tis like taking a piece of wilderness to convert into a field. Many a hard knock and heavy loss be requisite in the one and many head-aching and brain-perplexing hours must be spent in the other."[55]

What separated Belknap from his fellow historians were his high standards as a scholar. As a modern commentator has written, his standards "were a guide to excellence" for those who followed in his footsteps."[56] For Belknap, the writing of history began with a painstaking examination of all relevant sources. A connoisseur of caution, he placed an inordinate stress on thoroughness; he would take no shortcuts to Truth. Just as Alexander Pope aimed to be a correct poet, Belknap aimed to be a correct historian.

Belknap underscored this principle in a reply to Mathew Carey, the deeply patriotic and highly successful Philadelphia magazine

tive to history and having no liking for the subject. A recent revisionist study argues persuasively that Johnson has been misunderstood and misread, that he actually had a keen "sense of history." See John A. Vance, *Samuel Johnson and the Sense of History* (Athens, Ga., 1984).

54. Belknap to Hazard, Jan. 13, 1784, Mass. Hist. Soc., *Coll.*, 5th ser., 2:294-295.

55. Quoted in Daniell, "Belknap and The History of New Hampshire," 253.

56. Kraus, *Writing of American History*, 76.

publisher known as the "wild Irishman," who sought to hire him in 1787 to prepare articles on American geography, biography, and natural history. Belknap set forth his methodology for preparing this type of publication.

From the little experience I have had of historical writing, I should suppose as proper a method as any would be this: that collection be made of all the public newspapers, journals, pamphlets, plans, and drawings that may be published from time to time in each State, or in foreign countries relative to America, and your compiler furnished with them; that he should select such facts and observations as are worth preserving from *them*, and enter them in a memorandum with references. In that case a number of queries will arise in his mind which he will wish to pursue in order to gain a more clear and particular knowledge than can generally be had by publications of the common sort. To solve doubts and difficulties which may thus arise, and pursue enquiries into matters but superficially known, it would be proper that he should have some intelligent and faithful correspondent in each of the States to whom he may apply, and from whom he may expect a regular and seasonable return. Then his judgment and industry ought to guide him in forming his disposition and executing the work.[57]

For Belknap, accuracy and thoroughness took precedence over the passion for publication. Time was of no consequence. The critical issue was standards. As he informed Carey, he could easily write the requested articles on the basis of "some materials which I can now command." But he could not, in good conscience, function in this manner: "It might be an easy matter with writers of a certain sort to dish up a fricasee of newspaper intelligence and dignify it with the pompous title of The History of the United States. But a person who values his reputation as a writer would chuse to have the *best* materials, and even then would hesitate about many things which an inconsiderate scribler would venture to throw out at random."[58]

"A person who values his reputation"—this phrase appears frequently in Belknap's correspondence. He was preoccupied with this concern. "Zealous as I am to serve the cause of science," he wrote,

57. Belknap to Carey, Boston, May 18, 1787, Mass. Hist. Soc., *Coll.*, 6th ser., 4:336-337.

58. *Ibid.*, 337.

"I consider my reputation as at stake the moment I consent to undertake the work. The magnitude of the objects, the difficulty of obtaining the knowledge which an historian ought to be possessed of, and the time that must be employed in the work are discouraging circumstances."[59]

In 1842, Harper and Brothers, then one of the major publishers in the nation, produced a new edition of *American Biography*. Writing in the third person, Fordyce M. Hubbard, the editor of the project, who checked the sources used in the original work, rendered this laudatory report on Belknap's scrupulous scholarship:

He has re-examined all the statements of facts made by Dr. Belknap, and compared them with the authorities he used, and with others which were not accessible when he wrote. It has been very seldom that he has found occasion to differ from Dr. Belknap, and that most frequently in cases in which documents recently discovered have thrown light upon subjects which the want of them rendered necessarily obscure. It is believed that no work has been published of such magnitude, embracing such a variety of persons and events, and extending over a period of more than six hundred years, in which so few, and those so unimportant, errors are to be found. The manuscript collections yet remaining, from which the work was originally written, prove a degree of careful diligence, and a discriminating and impartial judgment, which have been rarely exercised by the historical inquirer.[60]

Belknap's fastidiousness as a scholar is further illustrated by the experience he had with Hazard in 1784. While editing the manuscript of Belknap's *History of New Hampshire*, Hazard advised him to cite a particular document relative to Thomas Hutchinson. Hazard was familiar with the document. But Belknap had not seen this source, and he was reluctant to cite it: "I am content you should refer to the Records which were his source, if you think it consistent with honesty to quote what I have not seen: there are some references to his collection of papers, which it may be best to adhere to, as they are public."[61] Hazard reassured him that "there is nothing

59. *Ibid.*

60. 1: vii.

61. Belknap to Hazard, Portsmouth, Apr. 30, 1784, Mass. Hist. Soc., *Coll.*, 5th ser., 2: 334.

inconsistent with either 'honesty' or morality in quoting records which *you* have never seen, if they are fairly quoted. Indeed, in this case *you have seen* them; for *I* saw them for you, and the law says, *'qui facit per alium facit per se'*; ergo. I would always choose to go to the fountain-head, when it could be done."[62]

Because he insisted upon high standards and valued his reputation, Belknap refused to concoct hasty history. He was contemptuous of those who haphazardly assembled their data and rushed into print. It took him "off and on nine or ten years" to complete his first volume of the history of New Hampshire. When his friend Hazard good humoredly twitted him on his slow pace, Belknap sternly replied: "I know that it might be run through in a much shorter time by a Grub Street Gazetteer, who would take every thing on trust, and had materials ready prepared."[63] Belknap refused to take anything on trust. He canvassed all available evidence before he placed quill to paper and sought to reconstruct the past.[64] He also cross-checked his sources. Witness his approach to discussing the Indian wars in his *History of New Hampshire*. "Mr. Hubbard, Dr. Mather and Mr. Penhallow have published narratives of the several Indian wars: These have been compared with the public records, with ancient manuscripts, with Charlevoix's history of New-France, and with the verbal traditions of the immediate sufferers or their descendants."[65] After notifying Ebenezer Hazard to collect all the gleanings of information "which can be had," he added these salient words: "For while any source is unexplored, or unattempted—I shall not think my business done."[66]

When feasible, he relied on the witnesses of history for information. His experience with the deposed royal governor of New Hamp-

62. Hazard to Belknap, Philadelphia, May 17, 1784, *ibid.*, 343.

63. Belknap to Hazard, Dover, Jan. 13, 1784, *ibid.*, 294.

64. Note the numerous sources Belknap cited in *The History of New Hampshire*, 3: preface.

65. *Ibid.*, 1: preface, vi.

66. Belknap to Hazard, Boston, Mar. 10, 1790, Belknap Papers, Massachusetts Historical Society. In 1789, Belknap wrote Jedidiah Morse and criticized him for the errors in his maps of New Hampshire in his proposed geographical publication. He provided him with better sources. Belknap to Morse, Boston, Feb. 17, 1789, Hist. Soc. of Pennsylvania, Gratz Collection.

shire, John Wentworth, is a case in point.[67] In 1791, while preparing the second volume of the *History of New Hampshire,* which covered the period of Wentworth's administration, Belknap wrote to the former royal official, then serving as chief executive of Nova Scotia, and solicited sources and information. While serving as royal governor of New Hampshire, Wentworth had strongly supported Belknap's project, even to the point of providing him with documents.[68] The two men enjoyed a warm professional and personal relationship, notwithstanding their opposing political views.[69] They remained firm friends during and after the Revolution.

Belknap informed Wentworth that he would not "leave any method unattempted by which it is possible for me to obtain as complete a knowledge as possible of the persons and things concerning which I write." He planned to consult a variety of sources in developing his analysis of Wentworth's administration, but "I do most sincerely wish that I could converse with you on some of these various topics, because it is my intention and desire to give as candid an account of things as is consistent with truth."

Belknap forewarned the former royal governor that he could not remain a disinterested observer when he discussed the Revolution: "It is true I always was and shall appear in this work to be an advocate for the American side of the question." In this instance, Belknap's personal feelings were too strong to be bound by the canon of impartiality. Above all, he was an American patriot. But he was quick to add that he would not omit misdeeds committed by his countrymen, among them the "havoc of private property made by confiscations."[70]

67. The American-born Wentworth was appointed royal governor by George III in 1767 and served until July 1775, when military activities erupted.

68. See, for example, John Wentworth to Belknap, Portsmouth, Mar. 10, 1774, Mass. Hist. Soc., *Coll.,* 6th ser., 4: 47-48; Belknap to Wentworth, Mar. 15, 1774, *ibid.,* 48-49.

69. When Belknap was living in Dover, Wentworth asked him to take his nephew into his home as a boarder-student, but the minister declined the request because of his busy schedule and lack of space in his home. His father, mother, and sister were also living with him at this time.

70. Quoted in Marcou, *Belknap,* 190. When Belknap came to discuss the American colonies' growing problems with Great Britain in the 1760s in *The History of New Hampshire,* he lapsed into the first person plural. He felt constrained to explain his stylistic adjustment in a footnote: "Though it may be

Belknap had no respect for historians who distorted facts or accepted sources without rigidly applying the rules of evidence. For these reasons, he held a low opinion of his highly regarded contemporary, the Reverend William Gordon, the transplanted English Whig, who also wrote history in his spare moments.[71]

Gordon had come to America in 1770, when the fires of rebellion were beginning to crackle. Planning to live there permanently, he visited a number of sites in search of a pulpit. In 1772, he settled in the Boston area. He became minister of the Third Congregational Society of Jamaica Plain in Roxbury, which was located a few miles southwest of the "City upon a Hill."

Like Belknap, Gordon believed that what was occurring in America was of momentous historical consequence. In 1775, as the controversy between the colonies and Great Britain reached the point of explosion, Gordon began collecting documents and data. He was "struck with the scenes that were opening upon the world." Viewing himself as an 18th-century Thucydides, he accelerated his collecting during and after the Revolution, soliciting information and documents from a host of prominent American political and military participants, including George Washington. In 1786, the minister-historian returned to England and began work on an account of the Revolution.[72] In 1788, he published a four-volume study which created a considerable stir in learned circles, both in Great Britain and America.[73]

accounted a deviation from the proper style of history, for the author to speak in the first person; yet he hopes to be excused in expressing the feelings of an American, whilst he relates the history of his own time, and his own country." See 2:246 n.

71. On Gordon's career, see James S. Loring, "Our First Historian of the American Revolution," *The Historical Magazine*, 6 (1862): 41-49; Shipton, *Sibley's Harvard Graduates*, 13:60-85; "Letters of the Reverend William Gordon, Historian of the American Revolution," Mass. Hist. Soc., *Procs.*, 63 (1929-30): 303-308.

72. Gordon's return to England coincided with Belknap's departure from Dover. Gordon recommended Belknap "to his people." Belknap was interested in Gordon's former position and preached there on at least three Sundays but was not called. See Belknap to Hazard, Boston, May 31, 1786, Mass. Hist. Soc., *Coll.*, 5th ser., 2:435; "Letters of Gordon," 537n.

73. *The History of the Rise, Progress and Establishment of the Independence of the United States of America* (London, 1788).

Belknap, however, was not impressed with Gordon's scholarship. In particular, he found fault with his use of sources. He accused Gordon of accepting information at face value. As Belknap informed Hazard: "I have heard it observed of him that the first report which he heard he would set down as true; and, if anybody doubted his information, or had the same story to tell different from the manner in which he related it, he would say, 'Sir, I have it from the best authority.'"[74] To Belknap, this was flawed scholarship.

Belknap constantly strove to locate the most credible authority. For him, the quality of historical writing depended on the quality of sources cited. And the greater the use of primary sources, or "fresh materials," the greater the possibility of historical accuracy. He constantly sought original sources, and he used them, profusely and proficiently. His appetite for manuscripts was insatiable. He would have approved of Mary Beard's aphorism: "no documents, no history."

Many, if not most, of Belknap's contemporaries tended to use information collected and published by others rather than search for it themselves. A common source for authors was the London publication, *Annual Register*, which Robert Dodsley began in 1758 and for which Edmund Burke served as editor for nearly 30 years.[75] This work was a compendium of parliamentary debates, trade statistics, book reviews, and assorted other information. For a time, it ran a

74. Belknap to Hazard, Boston, Aug. 19, 1789, Mass. Hist. Soc., *Coll.*, 5th ser., 3:159. Belknap found many other faults with Gordon's historical form and style. He noted: "There is a great collection of matter, indeed, in Gordon's work; but there are many things which are below the dignity of history to notice. Of what consequence is it that General Sullivan lived upon salted tongues and eggs in his Indian expedition? or that General Jo[seph] Warren was thought handsome by the ladies? But I will not attempt to point out blemishes. I only wish that Dr. Gordon had let his History be seen by some judicious friends, who were well acquainted with facts, before he left this country. I am persuaded that he might have profited by their advice; but he had too much of the self-sufficient principle in him." See Belknap to Hazard, Boston, July 18, 1789, *ibid.*, 151-152. Clifford Shipton has theorized that Belknap's displeasure with Gordon transcended scholarship. There was also the factor of jealousy. Shipton claims Belknap was piqued because Gordon had amassed a huge body of manuscripts from American participants of the Revolution, perhaps to take home to England. Shipton, *Sibley's Harvard Graduates*, 13:79.

75. See Thomas W. Copeland, "Burke and Dodsley's *Annual Register*," *Publications of the Modern Language Association of America*, 55 (1939): 223-245.

series of articles under the title, "History of Europe." These described important events in England and America relative to the Revolutionary War.

This segment of the *Annual Register* became the prime source for British and colonial authors who wrote about the Anglo-American conflict. It was common practice for these writers to copy information from the *Annual Register* verbatim. Gordon did this at length, as Orin G. Libby discovered a century later. In a preface to his *History*, Gordon wrote that the *Annual Register* had "been of service to the compiler of the present work," and that he had frequently quoted from it and other publications "without varying the language except for method and conciseness." Through the use of parallel texts, Libby conclusively proved that Gordon had done little more than copy information from the *Annual Register*. On this basis, he castigated Gordon's *History* as "one of the most complete plagiarisms on record."[76]

Libby also discovered that David Ramsay committed a double literary sin since, in his major works on the history of South Carolina and the Revolution, he plagiarized both Gordon's *History* and the *Annual Register*.[77] Libby wrote off both authors as intellectual frauds: "Our conclusion regarding both Ramsay and Gordon must be that they are no longer authorities at first hand, but are merely discredited and doubtful contemporaries, whose accounts must be severely tested before being taken for truth."[78] For Belknap, on the other hand, plagiarism was foreign to his method and alien to his values as an historian. He refused to engage in this type of shoddy scholarship.

76. Orin G. Libby, "A Critical Examination of Gordon's History of the American Revolution," American Historical Association, *Annual Report*, 1 (1900): 365-388. Clifford Shipton has written that Libby's condemnation of Gordon was unfair, since "Gordon frankly stated his indebtedness to the *Register*, which he used chiefly where he could not possibly have obtained access to manuscript sources. The History is a fair, strongly Whiggish account of the war, still useful for the areas in which he had first-hand knowledge, and denounced by his contemporaries because he pointed out the places in which the conduct of the Whigs fell short of their ideals." Shipton, *Sibley's Harvard Graduates*, 13: 81-82.

77. Libby, "Ramsay as a Plagiarist," *American Historical Review*, 7 (1902): 697-703.

78. *Ibid.*, 703.

In addition to scanning original sources, Belknap also interviewed elderly participants in, or witnesses to, historical events. After describing a battle with Indians in 1725, in his *History of New Hampshire*, Belknap noted that, along with primary and secondary sources, he had relied on the "verbal information of aged and intelligent persons."[79] In numerous other instances he cited informants as his source. As one authority has noted, Belknap was able to "impregnate his pages with a feeling of the contemporaneity of the historian with his materials."[80]

Belknap also traveled to and examined the sites where historical events had occurred. To be a "true geographer," he once informed Jedidiah Morse, "it is necessary to be a Traveller."[81] He believed that the historian, too, must travel, walk the ground where history had happened, and gain a physical "feel" of the scene he would later attempt to describe.

A visit to Bunker Hill was an enlightening experience for Belknap. After closely examining the terrain in Charlestown, he concluded that the famous battle there was a most hazardous and imprudent affair on both sides: "Our people were extreamly rash in taking so advanced a post without securing a retreat; and the British were equally rash in attacking them only in front, when they could so easily have taken them in the rear." He added: ". . . I think it essentially necessary to an historian that he should visit the spot where any such transaction passed, and minutely examine every circum-

79. Belknap, *History of New Hampshire*, 2:59n.

80. These are the words of Sidney Kaplan. See "Belknap as Literary Craftsman," 29.

81. Quoted in Kraus, *Writing of American History*, 83. In 1788, while preparing his geographical publication, Morse solicited information from Belknap on Massachusetts and New Hampshire. Belknap was annoyed by the request. They were questions which required considerable research. He preferred to spend what spare time he had on his own research and writing. He advised Morse to travel through those states with the best map he could find and speak with "intelligent sensible people" and he would learn more geography in a week's time than he [Belknap] could furnish him in months. Belknap to Morse, Dover, June 16, 1788, Hist. Soc. of Pennsylvania, Gratz Collection. In 1789, Belknap was instrumental in securing a ministerial position for Morse in the Charlestown First Church, even though he was at odds with him on doctrinal matters; Morse was a strict Calvinist. See Joseph W. Phillips, *Jedidiah Morse and New England Congregationalism* (New Brunswick, 1983), 22-26.

stance. This I did in 1784, with respect to the battle of Pigwacket, where Capt. Lovewell was killed, and by means of it I conceived a more perfect idea of that affair than it was possible to collect from books."[82]

One further example illustrates Belknap's uncommon view that a researcher should inspect the site where history had happened before writing his account and not rely wholly on documents or printed sources. When tracing the journey of Bartholomew Gosnold along the coastal area of Massachusetts in 1602 in his first volume of *American Biography*,[83] Belknap relied entirely upon the English explorer's journal, which had been published in an abridged form in Samuel Purchas's five-volume work *Purchas his Pilgrimage, or Relations of the World and the Religions observed, in all Ages and Places, etc.* (1625).

In 1797, while writing his second volume of *American Biography*, Belknap joined some colleagues and journeyed to New Bedford, where they boarded a ship and sailed through the area Gosnold explored 195 years earlier. The fact that Belknap's health was in a state of rapid decline (he died a year later) did not prevent him from undertaking this arduous journey. Belknap carried with him an assortment of printed primary sources and early maps which pertained to Gosnold's *Journal* and had been written by Gabriel Archer, a member of the expedition.[84] As he sailed about, Belknap pored over these documents and made a careful comparison with the terrain he was viewing.

Perhaps the most significant event in Gosnold's four-week exploration was his attempt to establish a permanent settlement on one of the islands in Buzzard's Bay. Gosnold wrote that his party began a fort and storehouse on a small "islet" located on "a large

82. Belknap to Hazard, Boston, Aug. 19, 1789, Mass. Hist. Soc., *Coll.*, 5th ser., 3:159.

83. *American Biography*, 1:231-239.

84. David and Alison Quinn, the foremost modern authorities on 17th-century exploration of North America, assert that Archer's account, while not free of errors, is the best contemporary source for Gosnold's expedition. See *The English New England Voyages, 1602-1608*, ed. David and Alison Quinn (London, 1983), 504-508. Archer's account of Gosnold's voyage is printed in ch. 1 of this authoritative study.

fresh pond." The prevailing view in the 18th century was that the site of the settlement was a large island that Gosnold had designated "Elizabeth, in honor of their Queen," but which is now called Naushon.

Belknap and his party made a special effort to verify this episode. In his first volume, Belknap had accepted Gosnold's account at face value. He had written that there was a "large fresh pond" at the southwest end of Naushon which answered to Gosnold's description, but he noted that "there is no islet in the middle of it." He concluded, however, that significant geological changes "within the space of almost two centuries could have taken place."

On the basis of his inspection, Belknap knew that Naushon was not the island described in Gosnold's *Journal*. The actual site, he believed, was the island called "Cuttyhunk, a contraction of Poo-cut-oh-hunk-un-noh, which signifies a thing that lies out of the water." At the western end of this island, on the north side, Belknap observed a fresh water pond, about three-fourths of a mile in length, "and of unequal breadth." If measured in all its "siniosities," it would amount to two miles in circumference. In the middle of its "breadth," near the western end, was a rocky islet nearly an acre in size.

On June 20, 1787, Belknap and his colleagues went "to this spot." What followed was a moment of high adventure. As Belknap wrote:

The protecting hand of Nature has reserved this favourite spot to herself. Its fertility and its productions are exactly as same as in Gosnold's time, excepting the wood, of which there is none. Every species of what he calls 'rubbish,' with strawberries, peas, tansy, and other fruits and herbs, appear in rich abundance, unmolested by any animal but aquatic birds.

Then the dramatic climax:

We had the supreme satisfaction to find the cellar of Gosnold's store-house; the stones of which were evidently taken from the neighbouring beach; the rocks of the islet being less moveable, and lying in ledges.[85]

After completing his site visit, Belknap returned to Boston and prepared another account of Gosnold's exploration for his second

85. *American Biography*, 2:115.

volume.[86] He inserted this significant footnote at the base of the first page:

The account of Gosnold's voyage and discovery, in the first volume of this work, is so erroneous, from the misinformation which I had received, that I thought it best to write the whole of it anew. The former mistakes are here corrected, partly from the best information which I could obtain, after the most assiduous inquiry; but principally from *my own observations*, on the spot; compared with the journal of the voyage more critically examined than before.[87]

As a rule, Belknap preferred to write of historical events and personages of a bygone era. He had serious reservations about writing contemporary history. "It is something of a venture," he informed Hazard, "to write the history of *living* men and recent transactions."[88] He would have agreed with Sir Walter Raleigh's view on this issue: ". . . that who-so-ever in writing a moderne Historie, shall follow truth too neare the heeles, it may happily strike out his teeth."[89] After mildly praising George Minot's history of Shays's Rebellion (it was written "with candor, and in a pleasing manner"), Belknap affirmed that he preferred to write "of dead men and facts long passed, where there is no fear of galling."[90]

Belknap expanded his views on the subject to Mathew Carey:

To write the history of one's own time, and to write it at or very near the time when the events come into existence, is in some cases impossible, in others improper. Facts and transactions are often viewed through the medium of prejudice at first, but in a course of time those prejudices may subside, and the same person may view them in another light, and draw observations and conclusions of a very different complexion. Besides, the views and designs of the actors on the public theatre are often concealed, and a

86. *Ibid.,* 100-123.

87. *Ibid.,* 100n.

88. Belknap to Hazard, Boston, Aug. 2, 1788, Mass. Hist. Soc., *Coll.,* 5th ser., 3:55.

89. Raleigh, *The History of the World* (London, 1614), preface. In other editions of this work, there are variations of this sentence but the meaning does not change.

90. Belknap to Hazard, Boston, Aug. 2, 1788, Mass. Hist. Soc., *Coll.,* 5th ser., 3:55.

writer of the most honest intentions may very innocently give a wrong colouring to things, whereas time and accident may develop secrets and strip off disguises which it is impossible at first enquiry to discover.[91]

Belknap was certain that a perceptive historian was capable of uncovering not only the truth, but even the motivation of the "actors on the public theatre," provided enough time had elapsed and there was an abundance of credible sources. John Adams, one of Belknap's correspondents, and a public figure for many years, held a contrary view. He remained a doubter: "My experience has very much diminished my faith in the veracity of History; it has convinced me that many of the most important facts are concealed; some of the most important characters but imperfectly known; many false facts imposed on historians and the world; and many empty characters displayed in great pomp. All this, I am sure, will happen in our American history."[92]

Adams's skeptical view found no favor with Belknap. His faith in the importance and value of history never wavered. And the historian, the seeker of truth, would remain for him a noble figure.

91. Belknap to Mathew Carey, Boston, May 18, 1787, *ibid.*, 6th ser., 4:337.

92. Adams to Belknap, New York, July 24, 1789, *ibid.*, 438. Adams was responding to a request for information on his involvement in key historical events and the location of basic sources. In 1778, during the height of the Revolution, Adams frivolously wrote Mercy Warren that he planned to retire "and spend all my leisure hours in writing a history of this revolution. And with an Hand as severe as Tacitus . . . draw the Portrait of every character that his figured in the business. But when it is done I will dig a Vault, and bury the Manuscript with a positive injunction, that it shall not be opened till a hundred years after My Death." Adams to Warren, Passy, Dec. 18, 1778, Warren-Adams Collection, Massachusetts Historical Society.

CIRCULAR LETTER,

OF THE

HISTORICAL SOCIETY.

SIR,

A SOCIETY has lately been inftituted in this town, called the HISTORICAL SOCIETY; the profeffed defign
of which is, to colle&t, preferve and communicate, materials
for a complete hiftory of this country, and accounts of all
valuable efforts of human ingenuity and induftry, from the
beginning of its fettlement. In purfuance of this plan, they
have already amaffed a large quantity of books, pamphlets
and manufcripts; and are ftill in fearch of more: A catalogue of which will be printed for the information of the
public.

THEY have alfo given encouragement to the publication of
a weekly paper, to be called THE AMERICAN APOLLO;
in which will be given the refult of their inquiries, into the natural, political and ecclefiaftical hiftory of this country. A propofal for the printing of this paper is here in-
clofed to you; and it is requefted that you would promote
fubfcriptions for it; and contribute to its value and importance, by attention to the articles annexed. The Society

beg

CIRCULAR LETTER of the Massachusetts Historical Society, 1791.

JOHN ELIOT, by Samuel King, 1779. Collection of the Massachusetts Historical Society.

PETER THACHER, engraving from a painting by Edward Savage, 1785. *Records of the Church in Brattle Square* (Boston, 1902), opposite p. 46.

JAMES SULLIVAN, by Gilbert Stuart, 1807. Collection of the Massachusetts Historical Society.

JAMES FREEMAN, by Christian Gullager, ca. 1794. Courtesy of King's Chapel, Boston.

THOMAS PRINCE, by an unknown artist after a 1750 portrait by John Greenwood. Collection of the Massachusetts Historical Society.

COTTON MATHER, engraving by Peter Pelham, 1727. Collection of the Massachusetts Historical Society.

WILLIAM GORDON, engraving after a portrait by Charles Hayter, 1796. Collection of the Massachusetts Historical Society.

FROM 1791 TO 1792, the Massachusetts Historical Society had its first home in the Library Room of the Massachusetts Bank, predecessor of the Bank of Boston. Contemporary views of the structure do not exist; this likeness is from a 19th-century bank stock transfer form. N. S. B. Gras, *The Massachusetts First National Bank of Boston, 1784-1934.* Copyright © 1937 by the President and Fellows of Harvard College, renewed 1964 by Ethel Gras. Used by permission.

THE SECOND HOME of the Massachusetts Historical Society, from 1792 to 1794, was in the northwest corner of the attic of Faneuil Hall, here depicted in the form in which it remained until 1805. This view shows the northwest corner. *Massachusetts Magazine,* March 1789, frontispiece.

COLUMBIA-WASHINGTON MEDAL, 1787. The partners in the voyage of the *Columbia-Rediviva*, the first American vessel to circumnavigate the globe, gave a copper version of this commemorative medal to the Society at its sixth meeting, December 21, 1791. The Society later acquired silver and pewter versions of the same medal. Collection of the Massachusetts Historical Society. Photo credit: Bowers and Marena Galleries.

MASSACHUSETTS PAPER MONEY, 1722. The Society received these one, two, and three pence notes, its first examples of paper money, from James Winthrop at its fifth meeting, October 24, 1791. Collection of the Massachusetts Historical Society. Photo credit: Bowers and Marena Galleries.

A PROSPECT OF THE COLLEDGES IN CAMBRIDGE IN NEW ENGLAND, by William Burgis, 1726. William Scollay gave the Society a copy of a later edition of this engraving in 1795. When the Society attempted to repair Scollay's gift in 1880, it discovered this unique copy of the 1726 edition pasted underneath. Collection of the Massachusetts Historical Society.

T H E

American Apollo,

PART I.——Vol. I.

Containinng the Publications of the HISTORICAL SOCIETY.

INSTRUCTIONS *given by* WILLIAM SHIRLEY, *Governor of Maſſachuſetts, to* WILLIAM PEPPERELL, *Lieutenant General of the forces raiſed in New-England, for an expedition againſt the French ſettlements on the Iſland of Cape Breton.*

SIR,

THE officers and men intended for the expedition againſt the French ſettlements on Cape Breton under your command, being embarked, and the neceſſary artillery, ammunition, arms, proviſion &c. ſhipped for that purpoſe ; you are hereby directed to repair on board the ſnow Shirley Galley, captain John Rouſe commander, and by virtue of the commiſſion you have received from me, take upon you the command of all and every the ſhips and other veſſels whether tranſports or cruizers of this and the neighbouring Provinces that are appointed for this ſervice ; and of all the troops raiſed for the fame ſervice, by this or any other of the neighbouring governments ; and to proceed with the ſaid veſſels and forces, wind and weather permitting, to Canſo, which place it is abſolutely neceſſary ſhould be appointed a rendezvous for the fleet. On your arrival there, you are to order two companies conſiſting of forty men each with their proper officers on ſhore to take poſſeſſion of the place and keep it ; appointing one of the two captains commandant of the whole ; which party is to have orders, without delay to land, and erect a block houſe frame, on the hill of Canſo, where the old one ſtood, and hoiſt Engliſh colours upon it ; encloſing it with pickets and palliſadoes, ſo that the ſides of the ſquare may extend
about

THE SOCIETY'S INSERT in the first issue of the *American Apollo*,
January 6, 1792.

❧ III ☙

Founding the "Historical Society"

Nil magnum sine labore (Nothing great is done without labor.)
Jeremy Belknap[1]

THE motives that inspired Belknap to found an historical society are easy to ascertain. First and foremost, his personal experience as a researcher confirmed the need for a central storehouse of reference materials. He fully understood the value of such a facility. In July 1789, Belknap began to read George Chalmers's popular work, *Political Annals*, which had been published in London in 1780. In a letter to John Adams, then serving as vice president, Belknap was envious of Chalmers's good fortune to be located close to his primary sources in London: "When I observe his [Chalmers] having had access to the papers in the Plantation Office, I feel a regret that an Ocean seperates me from such a grand repository—how necessary to form a just judgment of the secret springs of many American transactions!"[2]

Chalmers and other British historians had access to a number of grand repositories. In addition to the Plantation Office, they could pursue research at the British Museum, the Royal Society, the Society of Antiquaries of London, and the famous university libraries at Oxford and Cambridge. A number of imposing libraries were also available to scholars on the continent. French historians could work at the Académie des Inscriptions et Belles Lettres, founded in 1701, and Spanish scholars could conduct research at the Real Academia de la Historia, founded in Madrid in 1738. Other significant continental repositories included the Royal Library at Copenhagen, the Imperial Library at Vienna, the University of Göttingen Library, the Royal Library at Berlin, the Ambrosian Library at Milan, the Laurentian Library at Florence, and the Vatican Library at Rome.[3]

1. Belknap Papers, Massachusetts Historical Society.

2. Belknap to John Adams, Boston, July 18, 1789, Adams Papers, Massachusetts Historical Society.

3. Leslie W. Dunlap, *American Historical Societies, 1790-1860* (Madison, 1944), 4-5.

The American historian in Belknap's time lacked these advantages. Nowhere in the United States was there a repository that housed a body of reference materials. Nor could an historian conduct research on the activities of the national government. There was no federal depository or "National Archives" for public documents. The journals of Congress were regarded as secret information and were not available to researchers. The president and other principal governmental figures (as well as governors and chief state officials) treated their correspondence and business documents as personal papers and either carted them home or destroyed them when they left office.

There were only a handful of libraries in the nation, and none compared in size or importance with British or continental repositories. Outside New England there were only three libraries of note, and these were subscription organizations devoted principally to collecting *belles lettres*, not historical sources. The best known was the Library Company of Philadelphia, which Benjamin Franklin founded in 1731; he called it the "Mother of all the North American subscription libraries."[4] The Library Society of Charleston, South Carolina, established in 1747, and the New York Society Library, founded in 1754, also belonged to this category. The Library Company of Philadelphia was the largest of the three, housing close to 5,000 volumes in 1800.[5]

In New England, the most culturally advanced region of the young nation, there were only three libraries of any size or consequence: The Redwood Library in Newport, Rhode Island, which the wealthy businessman and book-lover, Abraham Redwood, established in 1747 as a subscription library; and the Harvard and Yale College

4. Benjamin Franklin, *The Autobiography of Benjamin Franklin*, ed. Leonard Labaree, *et al.* (New Haven, 1964), 130. Bernard Faÿ called it "the first great public library of the New World." See Faÿ, "Learned Societies in Europe and America in the Eighteenth Century," *American Historical Review*, 37 (1932): 258. See also Margaret B. Korty, "Benjamin Franklin and Eighteenth-Century American Libraries," *Transactions of the American Philosophical Society*, new ser., 55 (1965): 5-83; George M. Abbott, *A Short History of the Library Company of Philadelphia* (Philadelphia, 1913).

5. Charles C. Jewett, *A Report on the Public Libraries of the United States of America, January 1, 1850* (31st Congress, 1st session, Senate Miscellaneous Documents no. 120), 48-154, *passim*.

libraries, which were used almost entirely by students and faculty.[6] None of these repositories was amply stocked with documentary material or known as a center of historical research. Again, books were their staple.

The situation at Harvard deserves a word of elaboration. Until the evening of January 24, 1764, the college library, which contained over 5,000 volumes, was the largest in English-speaking America. On that bitterly cold and snowy night, the entire book collection, as well as college records and scientific instruments, was destroyed in a swift and spectacular fire. The authorities moved quickly to establish a new library and rebuild the collection. They were eminently successful in their effort. Although it sustained some losses during the Revolution, the Harvard library grew rapidly and by 1790 held over 12,000 volumes.[7] Yale, by comparison, had only 2,300 volumes in 1796.[8]

The two learned societies in the nation, the American Philosophical Society in Philadelphia and the American Academy of Arts and Sciences (Boston), were essentially organizations for discussion and publication rather than the collection of books and manuscripts. While broad-gauged in subject interests, they tended to focus on natural history. Their programs consisted of periodic meetings at which a company of "curious and congenial" savants presented and discussed papers. Their major activity was talk; as Bernard Faÿ has written of these men, "often they did nothing more."[9] Like their European counterparts, the American societies diffused "useful knowledge" through publications. They were not conceived as repositories for historical materials, nor did they treat history as a principal activity. Belknap became associated with both organiza-

6. For an examination of the libraries of the American colleges prior to 1800, see Louis Shores, *Origins of the American College Library* (Nashville, 1934), ch. 2; David Zubatsky, *The History of American Colleges and Their Libraries in the Seventeenth and Eighteenth Centuries: A Bibliographical Essay* (Champaign, 1979); Joe W. Krauss, "The Book Collections of Early American College Libraries," *Library Quarterly*, 43 (1973): 142-159.

7. John Eliot Alden, "Out of the Ashes, A Young Phoenix: Early Americana in the Harvard College Library," *William and Mary Quarterly*, 3rd ser., 3 (1946): 487-488.

8. Shores, *American College Library*, 52-53.

9. Faÿ, "Learned Societies in Europe and America," 258.

tions in time but found them only marginally useful for his historical work.[10]

Belknap's patriotism was another factor that led him to found an
historical society. An avowed cultural nationalist, he firmly believed
that the American experience was uniquely significant and would
alter patterns of governance throughout the civilized world. He particularly regarded the American Revolution as a special event in
world history. He shared the view forcefully expressed by Thomas
Paine in *Common Sense*, that "The Cause of America is in a great
Measure the Cause of all Mankind," that there never was a "Cause
of greater worth. It is not the affair of a City, a County, a Province,
or a Kingdom; but of a Continent—of at least one eighth part of the
habitable Globe."[11]

Belknap sensed the historical implication of the colonists' struggle
against Great Britain as early as June 1774, when the political crisis
was beginning to heat up. His personal papers for that month contain a draft of a letter to Andrew Eliot of Boston. While the letter
apparently was not sent, it nonetheless provides a revealing insight
into Belknap's thinking. He proposed that an effort be made to collect documents and printed materials pertaining to the Anglo-
American crisis and that these be stored in the Harvard College Library for the use of a "future historian." He elaborated:

If amidst the confusion and perplexity that now reigns through the whole
of our public affairs the still voice of Science may be heard I would beg
leave with all deference and humility to put her Votaries in mind that the
present Times exhibit so critical and important a Scene as must make a
distinguished figure in the Eyes of posterity and thence arises a necessity
that a properly authenticated Series of information impartially collected
should descend to them.

10. Belknap was elected a corresponding member of the American Philosophical Society in 1784. He was sponsored by Hazard; see Hazard to Belknap,
Philadelphia, Jan. 24, 1784, Mass. Hist. Soc., *Coll.*, 5th ser., 2:300-301. Belknap
was elected a member of the American Academy of Arts and Sciences in 1786.
See Walter M. Whitehill, "The Early History of the American Academy of Arts
and Sciences," *Bulletin of the American Academy of Arts and Sciences*, 24
(1971): 3-23. The Boston society was organized in 1780. John Adams was one of
the prime founders. On the title page of *The History of New Hampshire*, Belknap noted his membership in both societies.

11. *Common Sense*, 3rd ed. (Salem, Mass., 1776), intro., 12.

For this purpose I would submit it to your superior Judgement whether it might not be of advantage to appropriate some part of the College Library to the reception of such books and papers as may be presented for that purpose, and to recommend it to the Virtuosi of the present Times to replenish that Selected museum with such authentic Documents as may enable some future historian to delineate the present times in as full and perfect a manner as possible, and if some respect was had to past times perhaps the design might be better answered, as every person of observation must know that there are in the Libraries and Custody of Gentlemen of the present age many materials which are now neglected and which may soon be scattered the loss of which posterity may regret as much as we do now the carelessness of former Times.

And what precisely should be preserved? Belknap listed the following:

Political pamphlets, Newspapers, Letters, funeral and Election Sermons and many others papers which are now regarded only as beings of a day may if preserved give posterity a better idea of the Genius and Temper of the present age ⟨and of our most material Transactions⟩ than can be derived from any other source.[12]

Thus, while his fellow revolutionaries were intent upon making history, Belknap was preoccupied with the thought of preserving it.[13]

A third factor, as noted previously, was Belknap's concern over the loss of significant documentary sources through inattention, fire, natural disasters, and the "ravages of unprincipled or mercenary men."[14] "The want of public repositories for historical materials," Belknap wrote John Adams in 1789, "as well as the destruction of many valuable ones by fires, by war and by the lapse of time has long been a subject of regret in my mind. Many papers which are

12. Belknap to Eliot [Dover], June 18, 1774, Belknap Letter Book, Belknap Papers. Text in angle brackets was canceled by Belknap.

13. While the war was in progress, a few perceptive Americans began collecting sources on the conflict (Benjamin Rush and Joel Barlow, for example). Elbridge Gerry, a Massachusetts member of the Continental Congress, sought to pass legislation which would have required each state to designate an official who would collect and preserve "memorials" of the Revolution, but his effort was unsuccessful. See Michael Kraus, *The Writing of American History* (Norman, Okla., 1953), 89-90.

14. "Introductory Address from the Historical Society. To the Public," Mass. Hist. Soc., *Coll.*, 1st ser., 1:3.

daily thrown away may in future be much wanted, but except here and there a person who has a curiosity of his own to gratify no one cares to undertake the collection and of this class of Collectors there are scarcely any who take care for securing what they have got together after they have quitted the stage."[15]

In 1779, Belknap asked John Eliot to inquire among some Bostonians on the whereabouts of Lt. Gov. John Usher's papers. Eliot wrote back that one source stated that "he knew of none, and it would take him months to look over the rubbish where they must be if in existence."[16] This type of report greatly angered and dismayed Belknap.

Belknap was particularly distressed by the losses suffered in Massachusetts—and they were serious losses. He lamented the destruction of precious documents in the fire that leveled the court house in Boston in 1747, and the loss of the entire book collection in the conflagration at the Harvard College Library in 1764. While in sympathy with the American cause, he was angered by the sacking of Lt. Gov. Thomas Hutchinson's handsome home in Boston in 1765 by a mob of "patriots," and the consequent loss of a large body of valuable historical sources painstakingly collected by that royal official for his study of the Massachusetts Bay Colony. Belknap scourged the British forces who plundered the Court of Common Pleas as they were preparing to leave Boston in 1776 and scattered documents in the streets. And he was infuriated by the dispersal of the "greater part" of Thomas Prince's "noble collection of manuscripts" during the Revolution. These had been stored in the Old South steeple. Like most patriots, Belknap blamed the English soldiers for this "irretrievable loss," calling it a "sacrifice to British barbarity."[17] "Had we suffered it by the hands of Saracens," he wrote, "the grief had been less poignant!"[18]

The scattering of Prince's magisterial collection was the cruelest cut of all to Belknap. Aside from his close personal relationship with

15. Belknap to Adams, Boston, July 18, 1789, Adams Papers, Massachusetts Historical Society.

16. Eliot to Belknap, Boston, Sept. 11, [1779], Mass. Hist. Soc., *Coll.*, 6th ser., 4:149.

17. Belknap recorded this litany of losses in "Introductory Address from the Historical Society," Mass. Hist. Soc., *Coll.*, 1st ser., 1:3.

18. Jeremy Belknap, *The History of New Hampshire*, 3 vols. (Philadelphia and Boston, 1784-1792), 1: preface, iv.

the former minister of the Old South Church in his youth, he recognized the singular importance of these materials to researchers. He knew the collection well and had "frequent access to that library before the commencement of the late war."[19] He was a familiar figure in the Old South steeple. Even before the British had committed their act of cultural desecration, the collection had sustained losses and was in danger of being emasculated. Documents and books were disappearing and what remained in the Old South was poorly housed and in a disordered state. No one was watching over these materials.

This inattentiveness and the steady destruction of Prince's collection disturbed Belknap. In 1774, while researching his history of New Hampshire, he informed Lt. Gov. John Wentworth that he had hopes of traveling to Boston to examine documents in the Court House. He anticipated problems gaining access to these records because the Court would then be in session. He added these telling words: "besides all the time I shall be able to spare will be spent in searching the papers of the late Mr. Prince, of which there is a vast number lying in a most shamefully chaotic state."[20]

In June 1783, Belknap traveled to Boston from Dover to retrieve some documents he had arranged to acquire. He described the results to Hazard: "This day I set out homeward, with a grand acquisition since I have been here; viz., Governour Belcher's Letterbooks from 1732 to 1735. The rest have been (here you will join me in a sigh) torn up for waste paper. These are but 'scarcely saved.' How just the motto which I have chosen, *Tempus edax rerum*, etc."[21]

19. *Ibid.*

20. Belknap to Wentworth, [Dover], Mar. 15, 1774, Mass. Hist. Soc., *Coll.*, 6th ser., 4:49.

21. Belknap to Hazard, Boston, June 10, 1783, *ibid.*, 5th ser., 2:216-217. The Latin quotation is from Ovid's *Metamorphoses* 15:234-236:
    tempus edax rerum, tuque invidiosa vetustas,
    omnia destruitis vitiateque dentibus aevi
    paulatim lenta consumitis omnia morte.
    O Time, though devourer of (all) things, and thou, envious Age
    you destroy all things and (when) they are ruined by the teeth of Age,
    you little by little consume everything by slow death.
The passage is from a long discourse by Pythagoras on change and decay. With profound thanks to Mason Hammond, Harvard University.

What pained Belknap even "more severely" than the loss of such material was "the inattention of some persons in whose hands original papers have been deposited, and who have suffered them to be wasted and destroyed as things of no value."[22] He found it difficult to comprehend such irresponsible and insensitive stewardship.

The steady disappearance of primary sources led to what ultimately became an obsession with Belknap: the desire to publish all available materials. This one thought pervades his correspondence: "I am sensible that the only sure way to preserve manuscripts is to multiply the copies."[23] He was convinced that only publication would insure a sufficient supply of raw materials for future historians.

When Belknap returned to Boston from Dover in 1787, he met frequently with an old friend, Thomas Wallcut, a "zealous Antiquary" and extraordinary bibliophile.[24] The two men had much in common. Like Belknap, Wallcut believed that the only way to save valuable historical materials was to "multiply the copies." Wallcut's main concern, however, was rare books, his great love. According to John Eliot, Belknap frequently stated to him that Wallcut's suggestions for preserving books, coupled with "his [Belknap's] own desire to preserve the letters of Sir William Pepperell, were the foundation of the Historical Society."[25]

Belknap's difficulties in researching his study of New Hampshire

22. Belknap, *History of New Hampshire*, 1: preface, vii.

23. For example, Belknap to Hazard, Boston, Nov. 16, 1788, Mass. Hist. Soc., *Coll.*, 5th ser., 3:75. Thomas Jefferson also adhered to this view. On Feb. 18, 1791, he wrote Hazard from Philadelphia: "I learn with great satisfaction that you are about committing to the press the valuable historical and state-papers you have been so long collecting. Time and accident are committing daily havoc on the originals deposited in our public offices. The late war has done the work of centuries in this business. The lost cannot be recovered; but let us save what remains: not by vaults and locks which force them from the public eye and use, in consigning them to the waste of time, but by such a multiplication of copies, as shall place them beyond the reach of accident." Hist. Soc. of Pennsylvania, Ebenezer Hazard Papers. A facsimile copy of the letter is printed in *Documentary Editing*, 6 (1984), cover.

24. On Wallcut, see: Stewart Mitchell, *Handbook of Massachusetts Historical Society 1791-1948* (Boston, 1949), 3; Mass. Hist. Soc., *Procs.*, 2 (1835-1855): 193-208. Belknap called him "a genuine antiquarian." See Belknap to Hazard, Boston, Apr. 27, 1791, Mass. Hist. Soc., *Coll.*, 5th ser., 3:253.

25. John Eliot, *Biographical Dictionary . . .* (Salem and Boston, 1809), 61.

convinced him of the need for a repository where an historian could pursue his research. When he decided to undertake the study (about 1770), he was faced with the problem of locating source materials. One of his first actions was to direct a letter to Samuel Mather, son of the famous Cotton, who had inherited his father's vast personal library. Belknap solicited information on key books he needed (Captain John Smith's *Voyages of New England,* for example). He also inquired if Cotton's library contained any "Letters or Papers of my worthy predecessor . . . whom your honored father mentions in the Last book of his Magnalia as having communicated to him divers things, relative to the Indian Troubles."[26]

Not having access to a research library, Belknap was forced to travel throughout the state to locate relevant sources. Such itinerancy was costly, difficult to arrange, time-consuming, physically exhausting, and frequently unrewarding.[27] Belknap knew that before a repository could be established someone would have to begin gathering documentary sources and develop a basic collection. He decided to undertake this mission.

As he traveled through the New Hampshire countryside collecting data, Belknap simultaneously accumulated documents and printed matter. He was an indefatigable pack rat. In 18th-century America, perhaps only one other figure was a more assiduous and successful collector: Thomas Prince. Unlike Prince, who began collecting as a youngster, Belknap did not take up this activity until he had settled in Dover and started his history of the province.

The first documents Belknap acquired came easily. He had befriended an officer in the New Hampshire militia, a Col. Nathaniel Sparhawk. The latter had married a daughter of Sir William Pepperrell, a principal participant in New England's assault upon France's vaunted Louisburg fortification in 1745. Pepperrell's daughter had acquired her father's correspondence with Gov. William Shirley of Massachusetts which related to that celebrated victory.

26. Belknap to Mather, Dover [late 1771 or early 1772], Belknap Letter Book, Belknap Papers.

27. The cost was especially burdensome. Belknap repeatedly petitioned the New Hampshire legislature for "countenance and assistance." See, for example, Mass. Hist. Soc., *Coll.,* 6th ser., 4: 301-302.

Learning of Belknap's interest in such documents, Sparhawk graciously offered them to him and, according to John Eliot, "expressed
a desire that he [Belknap] would deposite them in some cabinet,
where they might be read by others, and be useful in future." Since
there was no "cabinet" in New England, Belknap took personal custody of the papers.[28]

And so it began. As he accelerated his research, Belknap intensified his collecting. He visited public offices in search of materials. He
sent circulars to clergymen and "other gentlemen of public character." He traveled through the towns of the state, interviewing people involved in "surveying, masting, hunting and scouting; as well
as in husbandry, manufactures, merchandise, navigation and fishery," and soliciting documents from them as well.[29] He badgered
those who had held positions of authority in the province, from
Governor Wentworth to local officials, urging them to search their
holdings for important papers. He spent untold hours "in the garrets
and rat-holes of old houses," poring over documents.[30]

In his correspondence with friends, Belknap gave the impression
that he loathed the drudgery of searching for documents and engag-
ing in historical research. It was pure exaggeration. In reality he
relished it. This was sheer intellectual pleasure, high adventure.
When he set his eyes upon musty documents, he felt the excitement
of the explorer. He gave expression to this feeling of exhilaration
in a letter to Hazard in 1787: "Yesterday I was rummaging some old
pamphlets (an amusement which is to me what the opening a mine
is to some other people)."[31] And he was doggedly persistent in his
search for significant historical sources, as revealed by this oft-
quoted statement: "I am willing even to scrape a dunghill, if I may
find a jewel at the bottom."[32] Those who knew the pudgy parson
realized that he was not writing for effect.

Belknap was an incessant borrower of historical materials from

28. Eliot, *Biographical Dictionary*, 61.

29. Belknap, *History of New Hampshire*, 3: preface, 3.

30. Belknap to Hazard, Dover, Jan. 13, 1784, Mass. Hist. Soc., *Coll.*, 5th ser.,
2: 295.

31. Belknap to Hazard, Boston, Mar. 14, 1787, *ibid.*, 467.

32. Belknap to Hazard, [Dover], Jan. 8, 1783, *ibid.*, 178.

friends and associates. Frequently, he failed to return them, and eventually they were incorporated into his personal collection. Governor Belcher's letterbooks are a case in point. Saved at the last minute, these documents were lent to the minister-historian.[33] As Belknap informed Hazard, "they are only *borrowed* of the owners, and must be returned when I have done using them, or when called for."[34] Whether they were "called for" is not known, but it is known that he did not return them to the owners. Eventually, he donated them to the historical society he founded. It is hard to know whether Belknap's failure to return materials was due to a lapse of memory or because of his desire to preserve them and make them accessible to his historical fraternity.

After two decades of active collecting, the acquisitive Belknap amassed one of the largest and most important bodies of historical sources in New England, if not the nation. As John Eliot wrote: "No man had ever collected a greater number of facts, circumstances and anecdotes, or a more valuable compilation of manuscripts, which might give information and entertainment to all those who wish to know the history of their own country."[35] This collection later became a cornerstone of the Massachusetts Historical Society.[36]

33. Joseph Russell to Belknap, Boston, June 23, 1783, *ibid.*, 6th ser., 4:251-252. When Abiel Holmes inherited the bound volumes of Ezra Stiles's letterbooks, he discovered that the sixth volume of this set was missing. Years later, the Belknap family sent it to him; this was long after Jeremy's death. Holmes wrote on the front cover of the volume that it probably had been borrowed by Belknap. It was a proper supposition. See Edmund S. Morgan, *The Gentle Puritan: A Life of Ezra Stiles, 1727-1795* (New Haven, London, 1962), 46n.

34. Belknap to Hazard, Dover, Aug. 16, 1784, Mass. Hist. Soc., *Coll.*, 5th ser., 3:169.

35. John Eliot, "Character of the Late Revd. Doctr. Belknap," 24-25, in Transactions of the . . . Church in Long Lane, Federal Street Church Records, Massachusetts Historical Society. In 1790, Belknap requested from George Washington copies of his correspondence relating to the New York-Vermont border dispute. See Belknap to Washington, Oct. 25, Jared Sparks Papers, Houghton Library, Harvard Univ., Cambridge, Mass. There is no record that Washington honored this request.

36. A detailed list of books, pamphlets, and manuscripts which Belknap offered to the Historical Society is printed in Mass. Hist. Soc., *Procs.*, 1st ser., 1 (1791-1835): 18-22.

It is not known when Belknap first conceived the idea of establishing an "historical society." If he did not formulate the notion while residing in Dover, he at least recognized the need for such an institution while there.[37] But he knew that the New Hampshire community was not an appropriate site for such a society. Dover lacked a learned elite who would utilize or support an historical library. As for the general citizenry, Belknap regarded them as an unlearned lot. In private correspondence he branded them as ignorant and cited their "inveterate antipathy to literature."[38]

As suggested by the draft letter to Eliot in 1774, for a time Belknap seemed to think that the Harvard College Library was a likely depository for an historical collection. The library made a rapid recovery from the disastrous fire of 1764, and the college officials kept steadily building up its resources. Since it was recognized as the "nerve-center of letters and learning"[39] for New England, Harvard seemed the logical and ideal site for an historical repository.

Even before Belknap returned to Boston from Dover, some Harvard officials gave serious thought to instituting such a program. As early as May 1780, during the height of the Revolution, Harvard's overseers voted that the corporation should consider acquiring for the library "every thing that has been written, that is worth preserving, relative to the present controversy between Great Britain and this country."[40] Belknap noted in 1787 that, "some years since," the aforementioned William Gordon had proposed to the college officials that a committee be appointed to collect "written and printed materials, for the use of some future historian, and deposit them in the library."[41] The officials responded by asking Gordon to implement his proposal and organize the archival program.

37. Belknap did play a key role in organizing a "social library" in Dover. He informed Hazard that the library "is under my care, and which I am concerned to cherish and increase." See Belknap to Hazard, Boston, Nov. 7, 1783, Mass. Hist. Soc., *Coll.*, 5th ser., 2:273.

38. Belknap to Hazard, Dover, Dec. 21, 1783, *ibid.*, 288.

39. Lyman H. Butterfield's phrase. See Butterfield, "Bostonians and Their Neighbors as Pack Rats," *The American Archivist*, 24 (1961): 143.

40. Overseers Records, Harvard College, vol. 3:195 (1768-88), May 11, 1780, Harvard College Archives.

41. Belknap to Hazard, Boston, May 18, 1787, Mass. Hist. Soc., *Coll.*, 5th ser., 2:481.

It was a logical request. Gordon, a "bustling busybody,"[42] was then engaged in research on the American Revolution and collecting sources for his study.

Although Gordon accepted the assignment, nothing came of his plan. Clifford Shipton has speculated that Gordon's lack of action stemmed from two reasons, both of which related to James Winthrop, the college librarian. First, Gordon despised John Hancock with a passion and regarded Winthrop as a lackey of the Revolutionary War luminary. Second, Gordon complained to the Corporation that Winthrop was too arrogant and refused to open the library to foreign visitors.[43] Gordon returned to England in 1786 and the plan seemed to be a dead issue.

In 1787, Harvard renewed its interest in the idea. In Belknap's words:

Some of the gentlemen in the government of the College are anxious to revive the matter; and, if they put it forward, I shall expect that part of the business will fall upon me, for I have often experienced that, where there is much labour and little profit, I am not out of employ; and you know there is a set of men who, when they see a person willing to work, will always put enough upon him to do.[44]

Belknap's prediction proved accurate. He had recently settled in Boston after his disastrous Dover experience and been appointed to the Board of Overseers. The college authorities quickly "put it forward" and Belknap agreed to assist his alma mater.[45]

With characteristic zeal, Belknap applied himself to the task. He

42. "Letters of the Reverend William Gordon, Historian of the American Revolution," Mass. Hist. Soc., *Procs.*, 63 (1929-1930): 305. Gordon was a prickly personality with an abrasive ego. He created friction wherever he went. John Adams called him "an eternal Talker, and somewhat vain, and not Accurate nor judicious . . . fond of being thought a Man of Influence at Head Quarters." See *Diary and Autobiography of John Adams*, ed. L. H. Butterfield *et al.*, 4 vols. (Cambridge, Mass., 1961), 2:174.

43. Shipton, *Sibley's Harvard Graduates*, 13:75.

44. Belknap to Hazard, Boston, May 18, 1787, Mass. Hist. Soc., *Coll.*, 5th ser., 2:481.

45. As an overseer, Belknap was appointed to the committee that had responsibility for the library. Overseers Records, vol. 3:343 (1768-88), Harvard College Archives. The records contain skimpy information on the activities of this committee.

approached a number of men who were known to have important collections and urged them to donate their materials to Harvard.

One of his principal targets was his old friend Ebenezer Hazard, who owned and was seeking to sell a "curious collection" of bound New York City newspapers and pamphlets; he had 60 volumes of papers and 50 of pamphlets. "Such a collection," wrote Hazard, "would be valuable in a public library, and perhaps the funds of Harvard University will admit of such a purpose." He set a price of $6 per volume of newspapers and $2 for a volume of pamphlets.[46]

Belknap knew that Harvard did not have available discretionary funds to purchase Hazard's collection at his stated price, which he considered exorbitant. He beseeched his friend to reduce the figure substantially. He concluded one letter with an appeal that was designed to blunt Hazard's obvious enthusiasm for financial gain: "Let us cheerfully serve our generation while we are capable; for what else are we sent into the world for but to do good?"[47] But Hazard was not moved by such pious supplications. He remained firm in his stipulated price.

Belknap agreed to present Hazard's proposition to the college in his capacity as member of a committee appointed to "regulate the Library." He broached the subject, as he later informed Hazard, "and was listened to, it was allowed to be an object worthy of attention, but no body seemed in earnest about prosecuting it—say and do you know are 2 things."[48] Disappointed by the administration's failure to act, Belknap decided to present a memorial to the college corporation: "This will be bringing it on as a regular piece of business." His efforts proved futile. The college governing body took no action on his memorial.[49]

Through the summer of 1787, while the Constitutional Convention held forth in Philadelphia, Belknap worked conscientiously to gather materials for the Harvard library. By September, his enthusiasm waned. It became apparent to him that he was engaged in a

46. Hazard to Belknap, New York, May 12, 1787, Mass. Hist. Soc., *Coll.*, 5th ser., 2:478.

47. Belknap to Hazard, Boston, May 18, 1787, *ibid.*, 481.

48. Belknap to Hazard, Boston, July 14, 1787, Belknap Papers.

49. *Ibid.* The *Harvard Library Catalogue of 1790* does not list the items Hazard was seeking to sell in 1787.

futile effort. He became exasperated by the lack of interest, even in-
difference, of the College officials and governing board. He informed
Hazard that they were not men of action: "I imagine it would be a
long-winded, and perhaps ineffectual business, to set on foot a collection of dead materials for the use of a future historian. They acknowledge the utility of such a thing, and that is all."[50] By the end
of 1787 he abandoned the project.

One wonders why Belknap did not donate at least a portion of his
vast personal collection to Harvard to set a proper example and stimulate others to give. He made no contribution whatsoever. Perhaps
he sensed that the plan was doomed to failure.

It is interesting to speculate on what might have happened had
Harvard taken the initiative to develop an American history collection in 1787, when Belknap was eager to work on its behalf. In all
likelihood, the Massachusetts Historical Society would not have
been founded, and the Harvard library would have acquired the
great treasures of Americana which were later deposited in the Boston institution.

The failure of the Harvard plan apparently convinced Belknap
that his idea would never come to fruition unless he and his cohorts
took matters into their own hands and founded an independent organization. Attaching such a program to a college library, or any
other established institution, was neither realistic nor feasible. It
would have difficulties sustaining itself as an appendage.

For a brief period, Belknap held to the belief that there should be
a publicly supported repository in New England for historical documents, both governmental and private. As he wrote in the preface
of his *History of New Hampshire*: "The very great utility of a public
repository for such papers under proper regulations, has appeared
to him [Belknap] in the strongest light, and he is persuaded that it
is an object worthy the attention of an enlightened legislature."[51]
But he failed to pursue the plan, apparently recognizing that there
was no possibility that the General Court would appropriate funds
for such an enterprise. He eventually discounted it, returning to the

50. Belknap to Hazard, Boston, Sept. 29, 1787, Mass. Hist. Soc., *Coll.*, 5th
ser., 2:494.

51. 1: preface, iv.

view that a private institution was the only realistic solution to the problem.

Belknap "wished that a beginning could be made," but the time was not yet ripe.[52] Throughout 1788 and much of 1789, he and his colleagues were preoccupied with two weighty public issues: Shays's Rebellion and the ratification of the federal constitution. Belknap was caught up in the excitement of both these dramatic events.

A social conservative to the core, Belknap regarded Shays's Rebellion as anathema and strongly supported the state government's action of suppressing the revolt by military force.[53] He was elated when he learned that the "insurgents" had conceded.

No supporter of the Articles of Confederation, Belknap welcomed the federal constitution. He was convinced that the new instrument struck "at the root of such evils as we have suffered by the madness of *Sovereign* State Assemblies; and, if the Congress themselves will not adopt the same sort of madness, I wish they may have the power to restrain and controul all the 13 Sub-Sovereignties, and exercise such a government over the whole as 'that we may lead quiet and peaceable lives, in all godliness and honesty.'"[54] He became a leading spokesman for the pro-ratification forces in Boston.

Belknap's interest in the state ratifying convention was all-consuming, especially when the body decided to conduct its meetings in his Long Lane Church. The delegates, numbering nearly 350, had begun their deliberations in the Old State House. A lack of space, however, forced them to transfer the convention to the Brattle Street Church, a larger facility. But after only two sessions there, they de-

52. Belknap to Hazard, Boston, Aug. 27, 1790, Mass. Hist. Soc., *Coll.*, 5th ser., 3:231.

53. When the state dispatched troops to western Massachusetts, Belknap applauded the action. See Belknap to Hazard, Boston, Dec. 2, 1786, *ibid.*, 2:447-448; Belknap to his wife, Boston, Jan. 14, 1787, *ibid.*, 6th ser., 4:325-326. Belknap similarly approved the suppression by force of a Shays-like element in the Exeter area of New Hampshire in September 1786. He urged a "severe check" to the "riotous spirit" of the "rabble." See Belknap to Josiah Waters, Exeter, Sept. 24, 1786, *ibid.*, 315-316. On Shays's Rebellion, see George Richards Minot, *The History of the Insurrections in Massachusetts in the Year MDCCLXXXVI, and the Rebellion Consequent Thereon* (Worcester, 1788); Marion L. Starkey, *A Little Rebellion* (New York, 1955); and David P. Szatmary, *Shays' Rebellion: The Making of an Agrarian Insurrection* (Amherst, 1980).

54. Belknap to Hazard, Boston, Dec. 8, 1787, Mass. Hist. Soc., *Coll.*, 5th ser., 2:498.

cided it was "too large and high to hear one another, [and] they got tired of it."[55] They ultimately moved to Belknap's wooden church, which proved to be an ideal meeting site; it was, in Belknap's words, "light, sizeable, and convenient for spectators."[56]

With Belknap serving as the nominal host, the Convention held forth in the Long Lane meeting house from January 17 to the final session on February 6. Belknap was in almost constant attendance. Like James Madison at the Philadelphia gathering, he took notes of the debates; his document is now one of the prime sources for the study of the convention.[57]

The delegates voted on the "great question" on February 6, 1788, and ratified 187 to 168.[58] Massachusetts was the sixth state to do so.

55. Belknap noted the problem of selecting a suitable meeting place in his "Minutes of the Convention," which are printed in Mass. Hist. Soc., *Procs.*, 3 (1855-1858): 296-304.

56. Belknap to Hazard, Boston, Jan. 20, 1788, Mass. Hist. Soc., *Coll.*, 5th ser., 3:6. This is a newsy letter on the early doings of the ratifying convention. See also, Transactions of the . . . Church in Long Lane, Federal Street Church Records, Massachusetts Historical Society; tipped in between pp. 128 and 129 of this bound volume of documents is a note of thanks from the ratifying convention to the church for the use of the building.

57. Belknap's notes, while important, are scanty in details. The most comprehensive account of the convention is Brandford K. Pierce and Charles Hale, eds., *Debates and Proceedings in the Convention of the Commonwealth of Massachusetts . . .* (Boston, 1856). Also extremely useful are Samuel B. Harding, *The Contest Over the Ratification of the Federal Constitution in the State of Massachusetts* (New York, 1896); and Thomas H. O'Connor and Alan Rogers, *This Momentous Affair: Massachusetts and the Ratification of the Constitution of the United States* (Boston, 1987).

58. "For two or three days [after the vote], the town was over head and ears in joy—bells, drums, guns, processions, etc." See Belknap's Diary, 1788, Belknap Papers. After ratification, the town fathers changed the name of Long Lane to Federal Street and the church fathers renamed their institution Federal Street Church. See Rev. Ezra S. Gannett, *A Memorial of the Federal Street Meeting House* (Boston, 1860), 22. Also, one enthusiast wrote a song, "A Yankee Song," to the tune of "Yankee Doodle," to mark the occasion. The first verse went as follows:

> The 'vention did in Boston meet,
> But State House could not hold 'em,
> So then they went to Fed'ral Street,
> And there the truth was told 'em—
> Yankee Doodle, keep it up!
> Yankee doodle, dandy;
> Mind the music and the step,
> And with the girls be handy.

After ratification in the remaining states, there began the critical process of organizing a federal government and merging the two systems into the new political structure. Belknap was engrossed by these significant and highly controversial public issues. Founding an historical society became a matter of secondary importance.

Then, in August 1789, John Pintard of New York City came to Boston and Belknap's interest in organizing an historical society suddenly was revived. Pintard proved to be the catalyst for transforming Belknap's concept into reality.

Pintard was a fascinating figure.[59] Although only 30 years old, he was already one of New York City's most prosperous merchants and substantial citizens. His beginnings did not portend such an elevated station. He lost both his parents before he reached his first birthday. His mother died two weeks after he was born, and his father, a sea-going merchant, succumbed on a voyage to Haiti, the victim of disease.

Pintard was raised by his merchant uncle, Lewis Pintard, who took his responsibilities as a surrogate parent seriously. A firm disciplinarian, Lewis maintained a close surveillance over his spirited nephew. He saw to it that the youngster was properly educated. Pintard attended the College of New Jersey, now Princeton University, where he fell under the influence of President John Witherspoon, the transplanted Scotsman and Anglophobe. During his senior year (1776), the Revolution began. Pintard and fellow Whig students rushed off to fight the British, although they never saw military action.

After the Revolution, Pintard participated in several business pursuits but was unable to achieve notable success in any of them. Then, fate intervened. His maternal grandfather died and left him a substantial legacy. Using these funds, he embarked on a number of business ventures, including trading in East India and China, and achieved sudden and spectacular success.

59. On Pintard, see James Grant Wilson, *John Pintard, Founder of the New-York Historical Society* (New York, 1902); Walter M. Whitehill, "John Pintard's 'Antiquarian Society,'" *New-York Historical Society Quarterly*, 45 (1961): 346-363; Joseph A. Scoville [Walter Barrett, pseud.], *Old Merchants of New York*, 2 vols. (New York, 1863), 2:217-244; James McLachlan, *et al.*, *Princetonians* (Princeton, 1980), 3:89-99.

Eight years after he graduated from Princeton, Pintard wrote his college chum Elias Boudinot that his ambition was to become "one of the first characters" of New York City.[60] He achieved his goal in short order.

A "lively, chearful" man of boundless energy, Pintard became an active participant in a myriad of civic, charitable, and cultural enterprises. He was the consummate urban booster and encouraged others to follow his example. He constantly prodded his fellow citizens to contribute to worthy causes and perform services for the public good. His promotional efforts were unusually successful. As a contemporary wrote: "He could indite a handbill that would inflame the minds of the people for any good work. He could call a meeting with the pen of a poet, and before the people met, he would have arranged the doings for a perfect success. He knew the weak point of every man, and he would gratify the vanity of men and get their money, and accomplish his good purpose, without any of them suspecting that they were merely the respectable names and moneyed tools that Mr. Pintard required."[61]

One of Pintard's principal cultural pursuits was promoting the researching and writing of history. The impulse came from within. He had a "passion for American history" and aspired to be a writer of history.[62] He was an avid collector of historical works. Like Belknap and many other learned men of this generation, he was a zealous cultural nationalist. He, too, regarded the American experience as a special event in world history; it deserved to be recorded. To do the job properly, historians needed original sources. In words strikingly similar to Belknap's statements on the subject, Pintard wrote: "Without the aid of original records and authentic documents, history will be nothing more than a well-combined series of ingenious conjectures and amusing fables."[63]

Pintard also shared Belknap's concern over the disappearance and

60. Quoted in David L. Sterling, "New York Patriarch: A Life of John Pintard 1759-1844" (Ph.D. diss., New York Univ.), 121.

61. Quoted in Scoville, *Old Merchants of New York*, 2:237.

62. See McLachlan, *Princetonians*, 3:92; Pintard to Belknap, New York City, Apr. 3, 1791, Mass. Hist. Soc., *Coll.*, 6th ser., 4:490.

63. *New York Herald*, Feb. 13, 1805.

destruction of historical sources. During the Revolution, he was outraged when British troops pillaged the King's College Library in New
York City. The loss of these sources led him to consider founding an
organization that would assume the responsibility for collecting such
materials, thereby allowing the gentlemen-scholars of New York
City to pursue their research and writing. He had proposed the formation of an "American Antiquarian Society."[64] Merely for project-
ing this vision, he has been acclaimed by some later commentators
as the "Father of American Historical Societies."[65]

One of Pintard's main reasons for his trip to Boston was to meet
Belknap. He had become acquainted with Ebenezer Hazard from
whom he had heard glowing reports about the minister-historian.[66]
He also had read, and was impressed by, Belknap's history of New
Hampshire.

The meeting took place, and it was a union of kindred spirits. Both
men shared a common interest and spoke a common language. Their
conversation ranged across the cultural landscape. The two disciples
of Clio discussed American history and books and authors.

Pintard informed Belknap of his plan to "form a Society of Antiquaries."[67] Both men could agree on the need for such a special
institution. They were displeased with the two existing national associations of savants, the American Philosophical Society of Philadelphia and the American Academy of Arts and Sciences of Boston.
These organizations paid lip service to historical studies, but each
exhibited a strong scientific bent. "To promote and encourage the
Knowledge of the Antiquities of *America*" was an ideal embodied
in the purpose clause of the Academy of Arts and Sciences' constitu-

64. On Sept. 5, 1789, Hazard wrote to Belknap: "Mr. Pintard has mentioned
to me his thoughts about an American Antiquarian Society. The idea pleases me
much. We shall have the plan upon paper one of these days, and you will doubtless be made acquainted with it." Mass. Hist. Soc., *Coll.*, 5th ser., 3:165.

65. See, for example, Wilson, *Pintard*, 26-27.

66. Hazard wrote to Belknap on Aug. 27, 1789, and described Pintard in these
words: "Mr. Pd. is a lively, chearful man, who appears to me not to want under-
standing as much as he does solidity. I can hardly form a determinate character
of him in my own mind, and yet in some respects I am disposed to think favour-
ably of him too. I think him a singular mixture of heterogeneous particles."
Mass. Hist. Soc., *Coll.*, 5th ser., 3:162.

67. Belknap to Hazard, Boston, Aug. 10, 1789, *ibid.*, 157.

tion, but in practice this body tilted sharply towards science.[68] Having attended its meetings, Belknap was well aware of this inclination.

In 1785, while visiting Philadelphia, Belknap had a first-hand experience with the lack of historical interest among members of the American Philosophical Society. He expressed a desire to attend a scheduled meeting of the Society, but his host, a member, convinced him it would be a wasted evening. Belknap was informed that scarcely "six or eight get together, unless on some extraordinary occasion." The two remained at the host's home and, in Belknap's words, "we spent the evening (as he thought) much more pleasantly." Belknap later learned that his host's judgment was sound. Only five or six members had attended the meeting and "their entertainment was a piece that Dr. Franklin sent them, on a method to make chimneys carry smoke well."[69]

What would be the fundamental structure of their society? Unfortunately, neither Belknap nor Pintard left any documentation on this important question, but there can be no doubt that both men envisioned an institution modeled after the Society of Antiquaries of London, at least in general form and purpose.[70] Thus, it would be composed of "learned gentlemen" who had a proclivity for antiquarian studies; it would collect a body of historical materials and artifacts and establish a library and cabinet room; it would have scheduled meetings at which the members would discuss subjects bearing

68. The 1780 bylaws of the American Academy of Arts and Sciences are printed in *Memoirs of the American Academy of Arts and Sciences to the End of the Year 1783* (Boston, 1785), 1:xii-xix.

69. Jane B. Marcou, *The Life of Jeremy Belknap, D.D.: The Historian of New Hampshire, With Selections From His Correspondence and Other Writings* (New York, 1847), 117.

70. The most comprehensive and authoritative account of this institution is Joan Evans's *A History of the Society of Antiquaries* (Oxford, 1956); my historical summary of the London Society is heavily based upon this work. For a brief but useful survey, see F. Hugh Thompson, "The Society of Antiquaries of London: Its History and Activities," Mass. Hist. Soc., *Procs.*, 93 (1981): 1-16. Julian Boyd has written that Pintard intended to model his organization on "the famous Society of Antiquaries of London and its younger sister society in Edinburgh," but the source he cites for this assertion (Belknap to Hazard, Boston, Aug. 10, 1789, Mass. Hist. Soc., *Coll.*, 5th ser., 3:157) does not offer corroboration. See Boyd, "State and Local Historical Societies in the United States," *American Historical Review*, 40 (1934-1935): 12.

upon antiquities; and it would sponsor a publication program. Since both Pintard and Belknap were closely attuned to British cultural and intellectual life, it seems certain that they were familiar with the venerable London Society.

The first antiquarian organization in the world, the Society was founded in London in 1707 "by a few gentlemen, well-wishers to Antiquities." The leader of this group was Humfrey Wanley, a learned and clubbable gentleman of whom it was said "that he ate too little and drank too much."[71] Without formally organizing, these men met weekly at various taverns in the Strand and along Fleet Street. At the outset, their activities consisted of spirited conversation and drinking. At times, attendance at these convivial gatherings dwindled and the group neared the point of dissolution. Then a zealous antiquarian would surface (for example, William Stukely, 1687-1765)[72] and the body would experience a renaissance.

Two key developments in the 1750s portended a more stable future. In 1751, George II, "that not very intellectual monarch," granted the group a charter and became a founder and patron. Two years later, the Society acquired its first permanent headquarters when it took a nine-year lease on a house in Chancery Lane. It established a joint library-cabinet room in these quarters.

In 1781, while Belknap anxiously awaited the end of the American Revolution and brooded over his personal problems in Dover, the Society made another major advance. It moved into the newly rebuilt Somerset House, a "magnificent and noble structure," which it shared with the Royal Society and Royal Academy. With this move the Society suddenly became "both large and fashionable." In 1784, its membership swelled to 376. A member wrote in 1785: "The Antiquarian Society is conducted on a very extensive plan, and it is now become one of our most fashionable weekly rendés vous's. Instead of old square toes you now behold smooth faces and dainty thin shoes with ponderous buckles on them."[73]

Collecting, preserving, discussing, and disseminating antiquarian

71. Quoted in Evans, *Society of Antiquaries*, 36.

72. The career of this eccentric but remarkable antiquarian is recounted in Stuart Piggott, *William Stukely: An Eighteenth-Century Antiquary* (Oxford, 1950).

73. Quoted in Evans, *Society of Antiquaries*, 187.

information—these were the basic activities of the Society. The weekly meetings were well attended, the publication program was expanded, and the holdings of the library-cabinet room substantially increased. The Society had become a fixture on London's cultural scene.

Two more antiquarian societies were founded in the 1780s and both were carbon copies of the London association in purpose, social composition of membership, and program. A Society of Antiquaries was organized in Edinburgh in 1780 by the eccentric 11th Earl of Buchan, David Steuart Erskine; it received its charter in 1783. This organization began with ambitious plans but did not achieve the level of development of the London Society.[74] A Society of Antiquaries was also founded in Dublin in 1780, but it was a short-lived organization. In the caustic words of Dr. Joan Evans, a modern president of the Society of Antiquaries of London, the Irish Society "was laughed out of existence by Governor Pownall."[75]

Thus, when Belknap and Pintard had their meeting in 1789, the concept of an "antiquarian society," as distinct from a "philosophical" or "scientific" society, was well established in England and Scotland. In adopting an English/Scottish model, Belknap and Pintard were following a time-honored American tradition of building upon European precedents.[76]

74. On the history of the Edinburgh Society, see William Smellie, *Account of the Institution and Progress of the Society of Antiquaries of Scotland*, 2 parts (Edinburgh, 1782-1784); William Smellie, "An Historical Account of the Society of Antiquaries of Scotland," *Archaeologia Scotica, or Transactions of the Society of Antiquaries of Scotland*, 1:1-9 (Edinburgh, 1792); and Iain Gordon Brown's humorous and delightfully irreverent *The Hobby-Horsical Antiquary: A Scottish Character 1640-1830* (Edinburgh, 1980).

75. Evans, *Society of Antiquaries*, 179. Thomas Pownall had a long career as a British colonial administrator, serving as royal governor of Massachusetts and South Carolina and lieutenant governor of New Jersey. During the Revolution, he served in Parliament. He was intensely interested in antiquarian studies and was an active member of the Society of Antiquaries of London. See John Schutz, *Thomas Pownall: British Defender of American Liberty* (Glendale, 1951), 232, 272-275, 278-279.

76. While I am convinced that the Society of Antiquaries of London was the basic model for both Belknap's and Pintard's vision of an American historical organization, I have not been able to uncover hard evidence to prove my contention. In extant correspondence, neither man made a specific reference to the London society. However, Belknap's original title for his proposed institution

Long before there were formal antiquarian societies in London and Edinburgh, there were antiquarians.[77] The antiquarian tradition first began in England in the Elizabethan era and, in time, came to embrace two well-defined strands of scholarship: the study of documentary sources; and the study of visible antiquities—ancient ruins, monuments, and other physical remains of the past. This dual character was emphasized in the Constitution of the Society of Antiquaries of London. Its stated mission was "to collect and print and keep exact Registers under proper heads Titles of all Antient Monuments that come to their hands whether Ecclesiastic or Civil, which may be communicated to them from all parts of the Kingdoms of Great Brittain and Ireland, such as old Citys, Stations, Camps, Castles, Theatres, Temples, Roads, Abbys, Churches, Statues, Tombs, Busts, Inscriptions, Ruins, Altars, Ornements, Utensils, habits, Seals, Armor, Portraicts, Medals, Urns, pavements, Maps, Charters, Manuscripts, Genealogys, Historys, Deeds, Letters, Records, Observations, Illustrations, Emendations of Books already published and whatever may properly belong to the History of BRITTISH ANTIQUITYS."[78]

("Antiquarian Society") tends to strengthen the supposition that the Bostonian looked to London for his inspiration. The late Walter M. Whitehill, a close student of Boston's cultural history, wrote that Belknap's organization was "inspired at least in name by the Society of Antiquaries in London." See Whitehill, *Independent Historical Societies: An enquiry into their research and publication functions and their financial future* ([Boston], 1962), 5. David D. van Tassel also subscribes to this belief but goes beyond Whitehill. He has written that the Edinburgh Society was "a closer spiritual kin" to the Massachusetts Historical Society than the London Society, and he added: "In the course of his work, Belknap corresponded with members of the Scots' society." Unfortunately, van Tassel did not provide documentation for his assertion. See van Tassel, *Recording America's Past: An Interpretation of the Development of Historical Studies in America 1607-1884* (Chicago, 1960), 61.

In 1985, I made an exhaustive search of the libraries and archives of the London and Edinburgh Societies but failed to uncover a single shred of evidence linking Belknap directly to either organization. While Belknap maintained an extensive correspondence with learned gentlemen in the United States and Europe, including Great Britain, he apparently did not communicate with either the London and Edinburgh societies or with prominent members of these organizations.

77. For a penetrating discussion of this subject, see Piggott, *Stukely*, ch. I.

78. Quoted in Evans, *Society of Antiquaries*, 58. The constitution is printed *in toto*.

By the mid 18th century, the fascination of English and Scottish antiquarians with monuments, relics, and other forms of material culture, especially of the Roman period, had increased to the point where this aspect of antiquities became dominant. Archaeological investigation became the principal interest and activity of the London Society as reflected by its publication, *Archaeologia or Miscellaneous*. Those antiquarians who were deeply attached to documentary sources and the traditional historical approach to viewing the past dwindled to a minority.

Bitter feelings developed between the men of "learning" and the men of "taste." In 1788, an anonymous member of the former group dramatized the split between the two elements in a caustic article in the *Gentleman's Magazine*. Referring specifically to the Society's major publication, *Archaeologia*, the critic wrote:

He who looks into the Archaeologia for profound researches into the ancient history, laws, poetry, or manners, of Britain, will be entirely disappointed; and will find the whole eight volumes to contain only amusing fugitive papers, on ancient buildings, monuments, medals, etc. with a few indeed of more importance intermixed. The word *Antiquary* is so undefined, even at present, that we more readily understand by it a man who is fond of collecting, and commenting on, antiquities, than one who aspires to the important task of illustrating ancient history, laws, or poetry. . . .[79]

Since there were no ancient monuments in the young republic, Belknap, Pintard, and other American antiquarians focused their attention on documentary sources—manuscripts, public records, pamphlets, books, and the like. The only ancient physical remains to be found in northeastern America were a few primitive Indian monuments, but these artifacts did not excite Belknap and other antiquarians. As ardent cultural nationalists, they equated antiquarianism with the history of the United States, and in their view this epoch began with the settlement of America by the white man.

Although Belknap held extremely liberal views on the treatment of the Indians by the white settlers, for this era, and manifested a scholar's curiosity for their history and culture, he shared his generation's traditional bias on their relationship to the birth and develop-

79. *Ibid.*, 197.

ment of the nation.[80] He regarded the Indians as bit players in this extraordinary chapter of world history. The white settlers and their descendants constituted the main characters of the American experience. They were the creators of the remarkable new order. Thus, Belknap's antiquarian interest was centered on this group and their achievements. In this area, his thinking was of a conventional order and he remained a man of his age.

While they left no written record on the subject, both Belknap and Pintard were assuredly aware that their view of antiquarianism was more narrow than that of their English and Scottish counterparts. It was limited to the study of paper sources which related to the history of the United States since its settlement in the early 17th century. Both also maintained a peripheral interest in natural history and therefore believed that an antiquarian society should collect "specimens of natural and artificial curiosities."

Both Belknap and Pintard were energized by their conversation, as well as impressed by each other. "I consider the personal acquaintance with the author of the History of N. Hampshire among the happiest circumstances attending my visit to Boston," wrote Pintard to Belknap upon his return to New York City.[81] Belknap reported to Hazard: "I must correspond with him—he appears very friendly and I hope I shall not be disappointed in him."[82]

And correspond they did. Letters and "bundles of books" soon began to flow between Boston and New York City. They also kept each other informed on developments relating to their proposed historical organizations.

80. Belknap's strange mental compound of liberalism and racism, with respect to Indians and Blacks, is discussed in George B. Kirsch, "Belknap and The Problem of Blacks and Indians," *Historical New Hampshire*, 34 (1974): 202-222. After founding the Historical Society in 1791, Belknap did solicit information on "monuments and relicks of the ancient Indians," but his interest in this facet of American history was not deep-seated.

81. Pintard to Belknap, New York City, Aug. 26, 1789, Mass. Hist. Soc., *Coll.*, 6th ser., 4:447.

82. Belknap to Hazard, Boston, Sept. 3, 1789, Belknap Papers. Shortly after meeting Pintard, Belknap wrote to Hazard (Aug. 10, 1789) that the New Yorker "seems to have a literary taste—is very loquacious and unreserved—Do give me his Character." Belknap Papers.

Pintard was the first to take action. A few months after his return to New York City, he set his plan in motion. Concluding that he could not found a separate institution, he "engrafted an antiquarian scheme of a museum" upon an existing organization, the Sons of St. Tammany Society.[83] Pintard had been the mainspring in reviving this moribund body in 1789; in 1782, he had organized a similar Tammany Society in New Jersey.[84] It should be noted that, at this time, the New York Society was a fraternal, patriotic, and social club in character and purpose. It had not yet become a potent political organization.

The "sole purpose" of the American Museum, as Pintard's creation was named, was "collecting and preserving whatever may relate to the history of our country, and serve to perpetuate the same, as also all American curiosities of nature and art."[85] In a letter to Thomas Jefferson in 1790, Pintard emphasized the historical aspect of the museum by noting that the object was "to collect and preserve whatever relates to our Country in art or nature, as well as every material which may serve to perpetuate the Memorial of national events and history. . . . The plan is a patriotic one and if prosecuted may prove a public benefit by affording a safe deposit for many fugitive tracts which serving the purpose of a day, are generally afterwards consigned to oblivion tho' ever so important in themselves, as useful to illustrate the manners of the time."[86] Thus, the museum was designed to serve the needs of scientific as well as historical researchers. Because he needed the support of local scientific-minded residents, Pintard was willing to compromise on the museum's mission, but his avowed objective was to make one segment of the institution an "antiquarian society"—that is, a haven for historians. To this end, he stocked the museum with historical books and pamphlets, and he dunned friends and associates for similar contribu-

83. Pintard to Belknap, New York City, Apr. 6, 1791, Mass. Hist. Soc., *Coll.*, 6th ser., 4:491.

84. McLachlan, *et al.*, *Princetonians*, 3:92.

85. The "Laws and Regulations" of the museum are printed in Scoville, *Old Merchants of New York City*, 1:176-178.

86. Pintard to Jefferson, New York City, Aug. 26, 1790, Julian Boyd, ed., *The Papers of Thomas Jefferson* (Princeton, 1965), 17:352-353n.

tions. His appeal to Belknap produced a copy of John Eliot's translation of the Bible into the language of the Massachuset Indians, a
notable work of that period.[87]

But Pintard's gallant effort was doomed to failure for a number
of reasons, not the least of which was the sudden loss of his fortune
and his abrupt departure to Newark, New Jersey, in early 1792.
Just as he was on the verge of accomplishing his goal, he became
mired in critical financial problems. At an earlier date, he had joined
forces with a fellow New York City entrepreneur, William Duer, in
some highly speculative ventures and had countersigned one million
dollars' worth of Duer's notes. In March 1792, creditors called in all
of these notes and, in so doing, caused the financial ruin of both
men. Duer went to debtor's prison, and Pintard fled to Newark to
avoid a similar fate.[88]

When Pintard's massive financial problems surfaced, he under-
standably turned his attention away from the "antiquarian society"
program, and the project died aborning. The museum fell under the
control of the "remarkable" Gardiner Baker, "New York's First
Museum Proprietor, Menagerie Keeper, and Promoter Extraordinary."[89] Baker had been appointed keeper of the museum when it
first opened in 1791. He had no interest whatsoever in history. Under
his guidance, the museum was perverted into a commercial side-
show, and the antiquarian society concept was laid to rest.

In 1801, after eight miserable years in Newark, one of which was

87. Pintard to Belknap, New York City, Oct. 11, 1790, Mass. Hist. Soc., *Coll.*,
6th ser., 4:469-470.

88. Belknap was saddened by the sudden financial demise of Pintard, but his
emotion transcended friendship. Pintard had served as his New York City agent
for the sale of his *History of New Hampshire*, an arrangement that worked to
Belknap's financial benefit. "He was my bookseller in New York," Belknap informed Hazard, "and paid me immediately for the whole parcel of the 1st and
2d volumes which I sent him, taking the distribution entirely to himself." Boston, May 8, 1792, Mass. Hist. Soc., *Coll.*, 5th ser., 3:293.

89. See Robert M. and Gale S. McClung, "Tammany's Remarkable Gardiner
Baker: New York's First Museum Proprietor, Menagerie Keeper, and Promoter
Extraordinary," *New-York Historical Society Quarterly*, 42 (1958): 143-169.
This article also provides information on the founding of the Tammany Society.
See also, Lloyd Haberly, "The American Museum from Baker to Barnum,"
New-York Historical Society Quarterly, 43 (1959): 273-288.

spent in a debtor's prison,[90] Pintard settled his financial problems, returned to New York City as a permanent resident, and sought to pick up the pieces of his shattered life. While he failed to achieve the high status he had earlier held, he did renew his activity as a zealous promoter of good works, and the old flame of an antiquarian society flickered anew.[91] He had become disillusioned by the direction the American Museum had taken under Baker's forceful leadership. It was now a curio shop, not a center of historical research. Knowing he could not resurrect this program at the museum, Pintard decided to take a new tack, that is, found a new organization. On November 20, 1804, Pintard and ten other New York City residents met in Mayor DeWitt Clinton's office and founded the New-York Historical Society. His 15-year-old dream finally had been realized. His "own brat," as he referred to the Society in 1818, was now reality.[92]

But Pintard's creation was not the first historical society founded in the United States. It was the second. His Boston compatriot had achieved *his* goal more than 13 years earlier!

In the year following Pintard's visit, Belknap and his historian-friends continued their informal discussions on the organization

90. Pintard's year in prison was not entirely a wasted period. The energetic New Yorker renewed his study of the classics, reading Virgil, Horace, Shakespeare's plays, Dryden, Pope, Milton, and the works of Samuel Johnson, including his *Dictionary*, item by item. He also studied the Greek Testament, and legal, theological, and economic works.

91. Thomas Bender has written: "Between 1801, when he returned to New York, and the late 1830's, when he began reducing his activities, Pintard assumed active roles in such a large number of civic institutions that to list them strains credibility." Bender lists 17, and this is not complete. See *New York Intellect: A History of Intellectual Life in New York City, From 1750 to the Beginning of Our Own Time* (New York, 1987), 50.

92. See [Dorothy C. Barck, ed.], *Letters From John Pintard to His Daughter, Eliza Noel Pintard Davidson, 1816-1833*, 4 vols. (New York, 1940-1941), 1:119. In one letter to his daughter, Pintard referred to the New-York Historical Society as "the Bantling I have brot into the world and which alone I shall consider myself bound to cherish." See *ibid.*, 1:105. On the early history of the Society, see Pamela Spence Richards, *Scholars and Gentlemen: The Library of the New-York Historical Society, 1804-1982* (Hamden, Conn., 1984). Ch. 1 covers the years 1804-1857.

they planned to establish.[93] Aside from Belknap, there were four other genteel scholars in this core. All were Harvard graduates, members of the Boston gentry, and relatively young. Three were ministers.

One of these was the Reverend John Eliot, the learned pastor of the New North Church.[94] Thirty-seven years of age, he was Belknap's closest friend and principal supporter of the proposed historical organization. He and Belknap were "mutual helpers of each others' inquiries and labours" in historical matters.[95] Eliot could well be credited as the secondary founder of the Society. He maintained a vigorous professional and avocational life, yet managed to find time to father 11 children!

The Reverend Peter Thacher, the 38-year-old minister of the Brattle Street Church, also bore a close personal relationship to Belknap.[96] He had been a student of Belknap's when the latter taught in Milton prior to entering the ministry. Thacher had been deeply influenced by Belknap, whom he regarded as a "friend and father."

Thacher had a meteoric rise in his ministerial career. He moved from a small parish in nearby Malden to the most prestigious church in Boston and all of New England. Befitting his station, he was the highest paid cleric in the city, receiving a weekly salary of seven pounds and four shillings.

While still a young man, Thacher was no ordinary cleric. A witty

93. Belknap informed Hazard on Aug. 27, 1790: "When Mr. Pintard was here, he strongly urged the forming a Society of American Antiquarians. Several other gentlemen have occasionally spoken to me on the same subject. Yesterday I was in company where it was again mentioned, and it was wished that a beginning could be made. This morning I have written something, and communicated it to the gentlemen who spoke of it yesterday. How it will issue, time must determine." Mass. Hist. Soc., *Coll.*, 5th ser., 3:231. Hazard replied: "I like Pintard's idea of a Society of American Antiquarians; but where will you find a sufficiency of members of suitable abilities and leisure? Where will jarring interests suffer the Musæum to be kept?" New York, Oct. 3, 1790, *ibid.*, 237.

94. On John Eliot, see Joseph McKean, *Memoir Towards a Character of Rev. John Eliot, S.T.D., prepared for the Massachusetts Historical Society and Published in Their Collections* (Boston, 1813). See also Mass. Hist. Soc., *Coll.*, 2nd ser., 1:211-248; John Lathrop, A *Discourse . . . Occasioned by the Death of Rev. John Eliot* (Boston, 1813).

95. McKean, *John Eliot*, 6.

96. On Thacher, see Shipton, *Sibley's Harvard Graduates*, 17:237-247; "Memoirs of Rev. Dr. Thacher," Mass. Hist. Soc., *Coll.*, 1st ser., 8:277-284.

conversationalist and skillful orator and sermonizer, he stood out as one of Boston's leading lights. He also held high rank as a prodigious producer of progeny, falling one child short of equaling Eliot's impressive achievement.[97]

William Tudor, the fourth founder, was 40 years old and a successful lawyer.[98] He was trained in John Adams's law office and served with the American army during the Revolution as a judge advocate. Like the other founders, he was active in civic and cultural affairs in Boston and was a prominent citizen.

The final member of the group was 37-year-old James Winthrop, who served as librarian of Harvard College from 1772 to 1787.[99] "Jemmy" was a member of one of New England's most illustrious families and the son of the Harvard scientific luminary Professor John Winthrop. A strange but brilliant man, he failed to match his eminent father in achievement or reputation. He seemed to lack motivation. His mother once noted: "He looks upon himself as a person that was not to be employed in life."[100] He had a prickly personality and managed to offend many of the people with whom he dealt. His excessive drinking may have contributed to his unpleasant demeanor. His penchant for the bottle matched his love for books and learning. As Clifford Shipton has written, he was content to be "a gentleman of leisure, with a bottle at hand."[101]

It should be emphasized that three of these four men were also collectors of historical materials and, therefore, prospective donors to the proposed society. This may have been a secondary reason why Belknap selected them as founders. Among Eliot's holding was the manuscript of William Hubbard's *History of New England*, a prize

97. In 1770, Thacher married a widow who already had some children. He fathered 10 more. According to Clifford Shipton, Thacher had a "miserable marriage."

98. On Tudor, see Shipton, *Sibley's Harvard Graduates*, 17:252-265; "Memoir of Hon. William Tudor," Mass. Hist. Soc., *Coll.*, 2nd ser., 8:285-306.

99. On Winthrop, see "Memoir of James Winthrop," *ibid.*, 2nd ser., 10:77-80; Shipton, *Sibley's Harvard Graduates*, 17:317-329. Winthrop served as Harvard's librarian from 1772 to 1787. See Shores, *American College Library*, 269-270.

100. Quoted in Lawrence Shaw Mayo, *The Winthrop Family in America* (Boston, 1948), 235.

101. Shipton, *Sibley's Harvard Graduates*, 17:317.

item for any historical library. Eliot's father had recovered this significant document after it had been taken from Thomas Hutchinson's home by the "enraged mob" and thrown into the street.[102] Both Thacher and Winthrop owned papers of their influential families. Winthrop's holdings were particularly impressive. They embodied many rare books and a large corpus of manuscripts, including "bundles" of Gov. John Winthrop's documents. These were housed in a special room of a small building that was located directly opposite Jemmy's "Mansion house" in Cambridge. The room had been designed to resemble the early Harvard library. Some of the planning sessions of Belknap's group were held there.[103]

Belknap apparently intended to include Samuel Adams in his proposed society. His "Plan of an Antiquarian Society," in which he listed the men to be invited to the first meeting, has the "Hon. Sam Adams" at the head. For unexplained reasons, he scratched a line across the noted rebel's name and never invited him to participate in the organization.[104] However, after the Society had been established, Belknap did attempt to extract historical documents from Adams.

While not a member of Belknap's inner circle, James Sullivan also was avidly interested in the project and gave it strong support. Only his frenetic schedule prevented him from taking an active role in organizational meetings.

Sullivan was a singular figure.[105] Born of Irish-Catholic parents in Berwick, the District of Maine, he was fortunate to have a learned father who, although an indentured servant, could speak seven languages and eventually became a schoolmaster. The elder Sullivan also took on the duties of a lawyer and drew up wills and deeds for his fellow townsmen.

102. See Thomas W. Higginson, "Address," Mass. Hist. Soc., *Procs.*, 2nd ser., 6 (1890-1891): 277-278; William Jenks, "An Account of the Massachusetts Historical Society," *Coll.*, 3rd ser., 7:9; *ibid.*, 2nd ser., 5: preface, iii.

103. Shipton, *Sibley's Harvard Graduates*, 17:325.

104. Plan of an Antiquarian Society, Belknap Papers.

105. On Sullivan, see Shipton, *Sibley's Harvard Graduates*, 15:299-322; Thomas C. Amory, *Life of James Sullivan*, 2 vols. (Boston, 1859); Mitchell, *Handbook*, 4-5; "Biographical Memoir of the Honourable James Sullivan," Mass. Hist. Soc., *Coll.*, 2nd ser., 1:252-254.

The father supervised his son's education. James learned Latin and French and read extensively in the classics and the Bible. He did not go on to college, although Harvard did award him an honorary degree *ad eundem* in later years and placed him in the class of 1762, Belknap's class.

A man of incredible energy and speculative temper, Sullivan achieved remarkable success in every activity in which he engaged, whether legal, military, or political. In 1782, he took up residence in Boston and began to practice law. He settled in quickly, developed a flourishing practice, and became a pillar of the community. He engaged in a number of civic, cultural, and commercial enterprises and was active in politics.[106] In what few spare hours he could find, he read and wrote history, his principal avocation. It was his custom to awaken before sunrise, light the candle and fire in his study, seat himself at his desk, and carry out his research and writing. In time, he produced two creditable historical treatises: *History of the District of Maine* (Boston, 1794) and *History of Land Titles in Massachusetts* (Boston, 1801).[107] He completed a third study, a history of the criminal law in Massachusetts, but failed to publish it.

Belknap and Sullivan had been warm friends for years. Their mutual love of history bonded their relationship. When Sullivan settled in Boston, he joined the Brattle Street Church. Shortly after he assumed membership, the Church had need of a new minister because of the death of the eminent Reverend Samuel Cooper. Sullivan campaigned aggressively in behalf of Belknap, who was then suffering ministerial misery in Dover. As John Eliot informed Belknap: "You know Jemmy Sullivan. He pretends, and I believe hath, a high esteem of you. He tells me, with an air of very confidential friendship,

---

106. Sullivan served as attorney general of the commonwealth from 1790 to 1807. He ran for governor in 1797 but was defeated. He was elected governor in 1807 and re-elected in 1808. Originally a Federalist, he changed his political affiliation after 1795 and became an ardent follower of Jefferson and his anti-Federalist policies. During the gubernatorial campaign of 1806, he was dropped from the presidency of the Society, ostensibly because of his political transmutation. See *Independent Chronicle*, May 29, 1806. He had served as president since its founding in 1791.

107. Sullivan donated the royalties for these two works to the Society. See Sullivan to Massachusetts Historical Society, Boston, Apr. 14, 1794, Records of Recording Secretary, 1791-1813, vol. 1.

he will push for you at Dr. Cooper's. He desired me to make an accidental change with you, etc."[108]

A serious split developed in the congregation on the successor to Cooper. One group, led by James Bowdoin, urged the appointment of John Bradford (Harvard, 1774). A second faction advanced the names of several other candidates. Notwithstanding Sullivan's sturdy prodding, the parishioners did not select Belknap. After a protracted debate, they chose Belknap's protégé, Thacher, who, ironically, was then embroiled in a bitter salary dispute with his Malden congregation and was pleased to take the Brattle Street pulpit.[109]

On August 26, 1790, Belknap and his four associates held a meeting, presumably at his home, at which they agreed on a course of action. On the following day, Belknap took the significant step that was designed to transform idea into reality. He set forth on paper a "Plan of an Antiquarian Society." The new organization was to be comprised of "not more than *seven members* at first," and its purposes were to collect, preserve, and communicate "the Antiquities of America."[110] The eminent scholar Julian Boyd aptly described this document as "the charter of the historical society movement" in the United States.[111]

The "Plan," or prospectus, embodied some significant provisions which reflected the full dimensions of Belknap's thinking about the organization he intended to found and about "antiquarian societies" in general. In the proposed Society's collecting policy, for example, he established broad geographical limits. The Society would collect materials pertaining to the entire nation, to "America." Each member "shall engage to use his utmost endeavours to collect and communicate to the Society manuscripts, printed books, pamphlets,

108. Eliot to Belknap, Boston, Feb. 6, 1784, Mass. Hist. Soc., *Coll.*, 6th ser., 4:270.

109. See Eliot to Belknap, Boston, Dec. 30, 1784, *ibid.*, 278; Thacher to Belknap, Boston, July 8, 1785, *ibid.*, 302-303.

110. A facsmile of the original manuscript of "Plan of an Antiquarian Society, August, 1790," in Belknap's script, is printed in: Mass. Hist. Soc., *Procs.*, 1st ser. (1791-1835), 1: preface, tipped in between xii-xiii; and Mass. Hist. Soc., *Coll.*, 5th ser., 3: tipped in between 230-231.

111. Boyd, "State and Local Historical Societies," 16.

historical facts, biographical anecdotes, observations on natural history, specimens of natural and artificial curiosities and any other matters which may elucidate the natural, and political history of America from the earliest times to the present day."

Further reflecting Belknap's (and Pintard's) national orientation, he envisioned a network of societies which were to work in close cooperation. The Boston group was to write "gentlemen in each of the United States requesting them to form similar societies and a correspondence shall be kept up between them for the purpose of communicating discoveries and information to each other." Each society was to publish communications from time to time, and these were to be of a uniform size: "all publications shall be made on paper and in pages of the same size that they may be bound together and each Society so publishing shall be desired to send gratuitously to each of the other Societies one dozen copies at least of each publication."

In a letter to Hazard on August 27, Belknap wrote these laconic words about his document: "This morning I have written something, and communicated it to the gentleman who spoke of it yesterday. How it will issue, time must determine. If it should come to any thing, you shall hear farther."[112]

After the August 26 meeting there was a lull. On September 14, Belknap informed Hazard: "No more as yet about the Antiquarian Society. The gentleman who seemed so zealous . . . has been ever since overwhelmed with business in the Supreme Court; and I have not once seen him, for I seldom attend courts of any kind."[113] The overworked gentleman was presumably Tudor.

As the new year opened, the pace began to quicken. An organizational meeting was scheduled for January 24. In planning for this gathering, the five principals decided to enlarge their group. Whereas Belknap originally had projected a nucleus of seven, he and his colleagues decided to seek five others of similar historical bent. Each was to nominate one person. Like the Roman *decemviri*, ten stalwarts would lead the Society.

112. Belknap to Hazard, Boston, Aug. 27, 1790, Mass. Hist. Soc., *Coll.*, 5th ser., 3:231.

113. Belknap to Hazard, Boston, Sept. 14, 1790, *ibid.*, 233.

James Sullivan, then serving as attorney general of the Common-wealth, headed the list of additions. He was a natural choice. George Richards Minot was also selected.[114] He, too, possessed proper cre-dentials. A graduate of Harvard, he had published highly regarded historical treatises on the Commonwealth and Shays's Rebellion.[115] A third choice was the aforementioned Thomas Wallcut, an eccen-tric bachelor and passionate bibliophile.[116] He collected historical books and pamphlets as aggressively as Belknap collected manu-scripts.[117] The final two additions were the Reverend James Freeman, a 1777 Harvard graduate and minister of King's Chapel,[118] and Dr. William Baylies, a well-known physician of Dighton, who "delighted much in fictitious history."[119] All five agreed to participate in the enterprise.[120]

114. On Minot, see James Freeman, "Character of Judge Minot," Mass. Hist. Soc., *Coll.*, 1st ser., 8:86-109.

115. Minot's book on Shays's Rebellion, *The History of the Insurrection in Massachusetts*, reflected a pronounced Federalist bias. It was a popular work when it appeared.

116. In his adult years, Wallcut lived with his aged mother. After she died, his eccentricity became more pronounced. He was frequently seen talking to himself, and he began sitting in the Negro pew of his church. His last days were spent in an insane asylum.

117. In 1834, Christopher Columbus Baldwin, the acquisitive librarian of the American Antiquarian Society, obtained a large segment of Wallcut's vast hold-ings of Americana, mostly pamphlets and newspapers. Baldwin described Wall-cut as a "curious and indefatigable collector of pamphlets." See Baldwin, *Diary of Christopher Columbus Baldwin* (Worcester, 1901), esp. 315-325. The weight of the materials Baldwin selected for shipment to Worcester came to "forty four hundred and seventy six pounds." There were at least 10,000 pamphlets in this lot.

118. On Freeman, see Francis W. P. Greenwood, "Memoir of Rev. James Freeman," Mass. Hist. Soc., *Coll.*, 3rd ser., 5:255-271.

119. On Baylies, see William Baylies, Sketch of the Life of William Baylies, Miscellaneous Manuscripts, Massachusetts Historical Society (written by Dr. Baylies's son); Shipton, *Sibley's Harvard Graduates*, 14:552-555.

120. According to Conrad Wright, seven of the ten founders (he includes Belknap) were religious liberals or "Arminians," as they were called. See Con-rad Wright, *The Beginnings of Unitarianism in America* (Boston, 1955), 262. Clifford Shipton acknowledges that Belknap was a religious liberal but disagrees with those modern Unitarians who have claimed him as one of their own. Ship-ton asserts: "that is going too far." *Sibley's Harvard Graduates*, 15:178.

The second organizational meeting was held at Tudor's imposing house.[121] Eight of the ten were present. Baylies was away and Minot was ill.

The first order of business was to choose officers. Wallcut was elected recording secretary. Next came the selection of the president. Sullivan, a man of Olympian stature in Boston (he would be elected governor of the Commonwealth in 1807), was a unanimous choice. Tudor was elected treasurer and Belknap corresponding secretary. Thacher, Winthrop, and Minot were elected the "Annual Committee," and Eliot assumed the dual position of librarian and cabinet keeper. Thus, all eight men were assigned positions of responsibility. None was a paid position. While there is no corroborating evidence, it seems likely that the group had reached a decision on what offices each of them would occupy prior to the balloting. Certainly, the elections were not competitive.

They next turned to the constitution, which Minot and Sullivan had drawn up and circulated in advance of the meeting.[122] The preamble set forth the aims and purposes of the Society:

The preservation of books, pamphlets, manuscripts and records, containing historical facts, biographical anecdotes, temporary projects, and beneficial speculations, conduces to mark the genius, delineate the manners, and trace the progress of society in the United States, and must always have a useful tendency to rescue the true history of this country from the ravages of time, and the effects of ignorance and neglect.

A collection of observations and descriptions in natural history and topography, together with specimens of natural and artificial curiosities, and a selection of every thing which can improve and promote the historic knowledge of our country, either in a physical or political view, has long

121. Minutes of Jan. 24 meeting, Massachusetts Historical Society Archives. The key documents pertaining to this organizational meeting have been printed in Mass. Hist. Soc., *Procs.*, 1st ser., 1 (1791-1835): 1-5. Tudor's house stood on Prison Lane, now Court Street. It was a favorite setting for elegant social fetes. See, for example, Marquis de Chastellux, *Travels in North America in the Years 1780, 1781 and 1782*, rev. trans. with intro. and notes by Howard C. Rice, Jr., 2 vols. (Chapel Hill, 1963), 2: 496-499.

122. There are three manuscript copies of the constitution in the Records of Recording Secretary, 1791-1813, vol. 1.

been considered as a desideratum; and as such a plan can be best executed by a society whose sole and special care shall be confined to the above objects: We the subscribers do agree to form such an institution, and to associate for the above purposes.

The 12 articles of the constitution contained a number of substantive modifications from the provisions set forth in Belknap's skeletal "Plan." The most significant was the change in title. The "Antiquarian Society" became "the Historical Society." This change seems to reflect the determination of Belknap and his colleagues to make a sharp distinction between their group and the American Academy of Arts and Sciences in particular. The title of their organization underscored their intention to focus specifically on historical subjects.[123]

Membership was another critical issue. The number of resident members was set at a maximum of 30. Corresponding members were also limited to 30. The records are silent on Belknap's thoughts on the relatively sharp increase in membership. His basic position had been that the membership should be limited only to those who had a sincere interest in the organization and were willing to work in its behalf. Experience had taught him that many men were quick to accept membership in cultural associations, but few were prepared to contribute time, money, or materials to their welfare. Shortly after the Society was founded and additional members were being sought, Belknap admonished his colleagues to select only those disposed to become "active workers in that field; in order that it [the Society] should not be tempted to elect members for the sake of bestowing upon them *a feather*, and become pursy and heavy by numbers, with-

123. On Dec. 11, 1790, John Eliot wrote a letter to Benjamin Trumbull, the historian of Connecticut, in which he stressed the historical orientation of the proposed society: "A number of us in this town have collected Mss and books —and have lately formed a society which we have called the *historical Society*, because it comprehends every thing relating to this country—its antiquities, its history civil, natural, and ecclesiastical. We confine our attention here—and hence are we different from the Academy and other literary Societies. To pursue one particular subject is the only way of succeeding. We mean to confine our attention to this business of collecting things which will illustrate the history of our country." Boston, Abiel Holmes Papers, Correspondence, 1705-1829, Massachusetts Historical Society.

out proportionate activity, and power of progress."[124] In short, Belknap preferred "doers," not "joiners."

Because he had a symbiotic relationship with Belknap and was his close collaborator in founding the Society, John Eliot is an important source on the issue of membership. He and Belknap were of one mind on this matter. In a letter to Benjamin Trumbull, the historian of Connecticut, on December 11, 1790, Eliot emphasized what Belknap later underscored in his admonition to his fellow members: that is, membership should be restricted to a low number and each person selected, including the corresponding members, must contribute to the welfare of the Society. These men were not to be passive bystanders, merely basking in the honor bestowed upon them. Echoing Belknap's sentiments on the subject, Eliot wrote:

We have added five Members, and mean to increase our number still, tho' never to exceed 25—except we introduce some gentlemen *from other States*. Tho we wish such a *circle* was in every State of the Union. By making the number extensive, or very *honourable*, it may be less useful. By honourable . . . I mean such members as are chosen into other Societies mearly to do honor unto the institution, or to receive honour from it. Every person shall be under obligations to assist in the business of the Society.[125]

Membership entailed a modest financial obligation. The founders established an admission fee of $5 for resident members and set annual dues at $2. If a member paid an additional $34 after six months from his admission, he was exempt from further payment of dues during his lifetime. Corresponding members were not required to pay an admission fee or dues. This was to be purely an honorific designation. There were to be four stated meetings annually.

The constitution, surprisingly, was *sui generis*. It was not modeled after that of a similar cultural institution, such as Boston's

124. These were not Belknap's precise words. Josiah Quincy, whose membership dated back to 1797, recalled Belknap uttering this sentiment. Quincy spoke at the Society in March 1858. See Mass. Hist. Soc., *Procs.*, 1st ser., 3 (1855-1858): 346.

125. Holmes Papers. The bylaws adopted by the Society limited resident membership to 30, not 25. The second five members were elected in this order: Sullivan, Minot, Freeman, Baylies, and Wallcut.

American Academy of Arts and Sciences or the London or Edinburgh
antiquarian societies.[126] Cribbing from existing constitutions was a
common practice of this era. Eschewing this practice, Minot and Sullivan created a fresh instrument of governance that conformed to the
needs and circumstances of the new organization.

And so, Belknap's cherished dream became reality. "We have now
formed our Society," he informed Hazard on February 19, 1791,
"and it is dubbed, not the Antiquarian, but the 'Historical Society.'
It consists at present of only 8, and is limited to 25.[127] We intend to
be an *active*, not a *passive*, literary body; not to lie waiting, like a
bed of oysters, for the tide (of communication) to flow in upon us,
but to *seek* and *find*, to *preserve* and *communicate* literary intelligence, especially in the historical way. We are not, however, quite
ripe for action."[128]

126. I made a careful comparison of the Society's constitution with those of
the other three institutions. There are no basic similarities.

127. The Society actually consisted of 10, not 8, and was limited to 30, not
25. Belknap's arithmetical errors are inexplicable. The limit of resident members
was raised to 60 in 1794 and to 100 in 1857.

128. Belknap to Hazard, Boston, Mass. Hist. Soc., *Coll.*, 5th ser., 3:245. Some
months earlier, Belknap had asked Hazard if it were possible to found an Antiquarian Society in Philadelphia. Hazard replied (Jan. 14, 1791): "You ask me if
an Antiquarian Society cannot be established here. Perhaps it might, and perhaps the thing might be considered as falling within the Philosophical Society's
department. I can hardly judge of it, for my pursuits and engagements are necessarily so very different now from what they were formerly, that I cannot even
visit a man of science, as such." *Ibid.*, 242.

Laying the Foundations

A Society has lately been instituted in this State, called the HIS-
TORICAL SOCIETY; the professed design of which is, to collect,
preserve, and communicate, materials for a complete history of this
country, and accounts of all valuable efforts of human ingenuity and
industry, from the beginning of its settlement.

Circular Letter of the Historical Society (1791)

There is nothing like having a *good repository*, and keeping a *good
look-out*, not waiting at home for things to fall into the lap, but prowling about like a wolf for the prey.[1]

Jeremy Belknap

BELKNAP was fated to live but six and one-half years after the
founding of the Society. His health steadily declined during
this period, but it had little effect on his efforts in behalf of the Society. He lavished much of his dwindling energy—and spare time—
upon the fledgling institution. It became his new "hobby horse,"
taking precedence over his research and writing. No other founder,
officer, or member was as active in its program or as solicitous of its
welfare as he was, a fact amply borne out by the Society's records.[2]
John Eliot noted after Belknap's death: "The Historical Society have
lost their most laborious and diligent member."[3] As he had played
a primary role in inspiring and founding the organization, so he remained the principal agent in its formative years.[4] He was deter-

1. Belknap to Hazard, Boston, Aug. 21, 1795, Mass. Hist. Soc., *Coll.*, 5th ser.,
3:356-357.

2. The bulk of these records, including correspondence, were generated by
Belknap.

3. "Character of Belknap," *Independent Chronicle*, June 25, 1798.

4. Over the years, a few writers have mildly debated the question: Who was
the real "founder" of the Society? While recognizing Belknap's pivotal role of
leadership, they have also credited others (such as Wallcut, Minot, Sullivan,
Eliot, and Tudor) as co-founders. The argument is purely academic. All were
undeniably interested in the project and participated in conceptual discussions,
but there is overwhelming evidence that Belknap was the "master spirit." He
made it happen. Eliot readily acknowledged him as "the founder of their institution." See *ibid.* See also Samuel A. Eliot, "Jeremy Belknap: A Paper in Rec-

mined to make the Society a permanent and significant component of Boston's enlarging cultural and educational system.[5]

One of Belknap's immediate objectives was to develop a library, or "literary warehouse," as one of his corresponding members from Georgia described it.[6] When planning the organization, Belknap and his fellow founders had pledged to donate items from their personal holdings to establish a nucleus.[7]

Nine of the founders honored their commitments; only Baylies failed to contribute.[8] Taken *in toto*, these donations constituted a remarkably strong foundation for an 18th-century library.[9] The So-

ognition of the One Hundred and Fiftieth Anniversary of the Massachusetts Historical Society," Mass. Hist. Soc., *Procs.*, 66 (1936-1941): 106; William Jenks, "An Account of the Massachusetts Historical Society," Mass. Hist. Soc., *Coll.*, 3rd ser., 7:8; John G. Palfrey, "A Discourse: Pronounced Before the Society, Oct. 31, 1844; On the Completion of Fifty Years From its Incorporation," *ibid.*, 3rd ser., 9:166; Samuel Miller, *A Brief Retrospect of the Eighteenth Century*, 2 vols. (New York, 1803), 2:261.

5. See Walter M. Whitehill, "Learned Societies in Boston," in *The Pursuit of Knowledge in the Early American Republic: American Scientific and Learned Societies from Colonial Times to the Civil War*, ed. Alexandra Oleson and Sanborn C. Brown (Baltimore, 1976), 151-173.

6. Lemuel Kollacke to Belknap, Savannah, Dec. 4, 1797, Correspondence of Corresponding Secretary, 1791-98, Massachusetts Historical Society Archives.

7. Where were these materials housed? From its founding to Belknap's death, the Society had three "homes" in what is now the heart of Boston. From July 1791 to July 1792, it occupied the Library Room of the "Manufactory House," headquarters of the Massachusetts Bank. From July 1792 to June 1794, it was located in the northwest corner of the attic of Faneuil Hall, a site described "as retired and recondite as explorers into the recesses of antiquity could think of visiting." From June 1794 to the time of Belknap's death, it was housed in the upper room over the arch in the Tontine Crescent, an elegant complex of 16 connected brick houses arranged in the form of a crescent. Charles Bulfinch designed this building, which was located at present-day Franklin Street. It was demolished in 1858. On all of the Society's "homes," see *Here We Have Lived: The Houses of the Massachusetts Historical Society* (Boston, 1967).

8. In recording institutional developments from 1791 to Belknap's death, I have used Society archival sources (minutes of meetings, committee reports, correspondence) and a digest of these sources which is printed in Mass. Hist. Soc., *Procs.*, 1 (1791-1835): 1-117. Many key documents are published therein and the actions of every Society meeting are summarized.

9. For the lists of their initial donations, see *ibid.*, 6-13; Belknap's extensive gift is on 18-22. The men submitted lists initially and their materials subse-

ciety acquired hundreds of 17th- and 18th-century books and pamphlets and a sizable assortment of manuscripts, maps, and other types of primary sources.

Not surprisingly, Belknap made the largest and most significant contribution.[10] His manuscripts were of singular importance. They included: four folio volumes of Gov. Jonathan Belcher's letters, public and private, for the years 1731 to 1735 and 1739 to 1740; the correspondence between governors William Shirley and Benning Wentworth from 1742 to 1753; the correspondence between Shirley and Gen. William Pepperrell from 1745 to 1746; the correspondence between Pepperrell and Commo. Peter Warren during the campaign of 1745 at Louisburg; the correspondence between Pepperrell, Warren, and the British ministry in 1745, 1746, and 1747; the correspondence between Pepperrell and "many persons of distinction" in various parts of America in 1745, 1746, and 1747; the correspondence between Gov. Benning Wentworth and the British ministry and their military officers from 1750 to 1760; the correspondence between the secretary of New Hampshire and the provincial agent in England from 1734 to 1760; papers relative to the controversy "agitated" in England by Peter Livius against Gov. John Wentworth, 1773; papers relative to the change of government in New Hampshire in 1775; the correspondence of the Sons of Liberty from 1766 to 1770; several manuscript journals from the 16th, 17th, and 18th centuries; a collection of papers relative to Nova Scotia from 1720 to 1747; and ten cases of manuscripts containing letters from governors and other public officials, with "many curious MSS. of various kinds" from

quently. Some of them made additional gifts in later years. Stephen T. Riley, who served as librarian (1947-57) and director (1957-76) of the Society and was responsible for the acquisition of many major documentary collections, wrote in 1957 of these donations: "If some of the manuscripts given at that time were offered for sale today, there would be a considerable stir in the collector's world." "Some Aspects of the Society's Manuscript Collection," Mass. Hist. Soc., *Procs.*, 70 (1950-1953): 240.

10. In 1796, the Society published a *Catalogue* of its printed works. It listed 1,010 items. Belknap had contributed 171, or nearly 15% of this total. (I am indebted to the late Dr. John D. Cushing, the Society's former librarian, for these statistics.) The *Catalogue* did not list unbound books, pamphlets, or newspapers. Nor did it list European publications, unless they had a connection with American history. See Mass. Hist. Soc., *Procs.*, 1st ser., 1 (1791-1835): 103n.

1698 to 1761. In addition, he donated: a collection of Boston newspapers from 1707 to 1750; a collection of newspapers of Boston, Salem, Portsmouth, and Philadelphia from 1756 to 1790, "pretty near complete," and a parcel of old almanacs, proclamations, and other printed papers. He also contributed a large number of books.

While Belknap willingly donated these materials to the Society, he was not above seeking a financial benefit from his munificence. The founders had set life membership at 34 dollars. Belknap requested that a select portion of his donation be credited toward a life subscription. The Standing Committee made an appraisal of these items and assigned to them a value of "thirty-four dollars and one-third of a dollar."[11]

While Belknap's gift was voluminous by any standard, it was not the full extent of his personal holdings. On the contrary, he retained a substantial portion. In 1858, 60 years after Belknap's death, Miss Elizabeth Belknap, his sole surviving child, donated to the Society his remaining manuscripts, books, and pamphlets. Included in this vast accumulation were his personal papers and private correspondence.[12] Why he did not will these materials to the Society, especially the historical segment, is difficult to understand, given his enthusiastic interest in the organization and his passion for the preservation of documentary sources.

Once the Society had acquired a nucleus, its officers sought to enlarge the collection. Predictably, Belknap spearheaded this effort. With an almost evangelical zeal, he assumed the roles of chief collector and principal prodder.[13] He operated on the premise that the Society would be an aggressive "procurer." It should not sit passively and wait for materials to be donated. He expressed this principle of activism in these colorful and oft-quoted words: "There is nothing like having a *good repository*, and keeping a *good look-out*, not

11. *Ibid.*, 23. Belknap was the sole donor to receive this concession, which attests to the singular character of his gift.

12. For an analysis of this significant donation, see Charles Deane, "Report on the Belknap Collection," Mass. Hist. Soc., *Procs.*, 1st ser., 3 (1855-1858): 285-328.

13. The many letters contained in the Corresponding Secretary's bulky volume of correspondence for the years 1791-1798 (Belknap's tenure in this office) confirm Belknap's industriousness and exceptional commitment to this cause.

waiting at home for things to fall into the lap, but prowling about like a wolf for the prey."[14]

In December 1796, Belknap conceived a design for the seal of the Society which represented his belief that it should be an aggressive collector. The Society undertook to design a seal after the state legislature approved its articles of incorporation in 1794.[15] In December of that year, the members appointed James Winthrop a committee of one to create a design for the seal. "Troublesome" James submitted his rough sketch the next month. He proposed the following:

An antiquary sitting on a ruin, and copying an inscription from the pedestal of an obelisk. Beyond the obelisk appears an ancient wall and gateway, and behind the wall a pyramid. The ruins of a decayed portico appear before part of the pyramid, and are seen together with some scattered fragments of columns, behind the antiquary. The legend, 'Massachusetts Historical Society, 1794. E Vetustate Lux.'

Winthrop's proposal evoked a response something less than enthusiastic. After reviewing his design, the members voted "that the subject be referred to the next meeting of the Society; and that in the meantime, each member turn his attention to it."[16]

Belknap had been thinking about an appropriate symbol for the organization from the moment he founded it. There is a curious document among his personal papers, dated 1791, which related to a seal: "For the Historical Society a Beehive—supported by two Beavers Nil magnum sine labore Nothing great is done without labour." But he apparently did not prepare a sketch or formally submit his idea to his colleagues.

Belknap again turned his attention to a design in December 1796,

14. Belknap to Hazard, Boston, Aug. 21, 1795, Mass. Hist. Soc., *Coll.*, 5th ser., 3:356-357.

15. The Act of Incorporation is printed in *American Apollo*, Mar. 13, 1794. The General Court passed the bill on Feb. 19. A key provision was the change in name, from "The Historical Society" to the "Massachusetts Historical Society." By the act, members of both branches of the legislature were given "free access" to the library and museum.

16. See Stewart Mitchell, *Handbook of the Massachusetts Historical Society 1791-1948* (Boston, 1949), 7-8. A facsimile of Winthrop's "Report of a Seal for the Historical Society," which contains his "rough sketch," is in Mass. Hist. Soc., *Procs.*, 1st ser. (1791-1835), tipped in between 338-339.

after it had become apparent that Winthrop's proposal was a dead issue and that none of his fellow members was eager to submit an entry. He wrote in his diary: "Device and motto for a Seal for Historical Socy a flying *eagle*—a ranging *wolf*—and a *shark*—all seeking their prey."[17]

The symbolism was dramatic and starkly dissimilar from his earlier effort. Whether Belknap actually developed a sketch of his three predators "seeking their prey" is not known. Society records make no mention of one. What is known is that his design did not appear on the Society's seal. The issue was not resolved until 1834 when, acting upon a submission from President John Davis, the Society adopted the design of a bee and a hive complemented by a Latin motto of Virgilian derivation: *Sic vos non vobis* ("Thus you do, not for yourselves.").[18] It is not known if Davis's beehive drew its inspiration from Belknap's scheme of 1791.

One can speculate that Belknap would have approved Davis's symbolism. He, too, looked upon the Society as a facilitator of research. But, with respect to the Society's role as a collector of historical materials, the symbols of the eagle, wolf, and shark were more appropriate to Belknap. Not surprisingly, his office of corresponding secretary was the perfect post for one who held such ambitions for the Society.

When Belknap began his research on the history of New Hampshire, he used Thomas Prince's tactic of preparing a detailed questionnaire and sending it to "men of learning" throughout the state. Like Prince, he also achieved positive results. He amassed a considerable body of materials and information. With the formation of the Society, Belknap again used this technique. In November 1791, he developed, and the Society printed, a "Circular Letter of the Historical Society." In a prefatory section, he reported on the creation of

17. Diary, Dec. 1796, Belknap Papers, Massachusetts Historical Society. Near the end of his life, Belknap wrote down an idea for a "motto for my family arms." For the seal, he chose "three flying eagles and a chained tyger" and, for the inscription, he selected the Latin phrase: "sit tygris domitus, sed aquila per astra volabit"—which he translated: "Let *passion* be restrained within my soul / But Genius rise and soar without controul."

18. Virgil's complete line was *"Sic vos non vobis mellificatis apes"* (Thus do ye, bees, for others make honey). See Mass. Hist. Soc., *Procs.*, 1 (1791-1835): 483-486. The history of the seal is discussed in *ibid.*, 15 (1876-1877): 256-258.

the Society, explained its purposes, called attention to its growing collections, and announced the publication of a new periodical, *American Apollo*, which was to contain a supplement of historical articles prepared by the Society.[19]

The main portion of the document centered upon a request for basic historical information, which, Belknap affirmed, eventually would be printed in the *Apollo*. He listed 14 subject areas for which he solicited information. They ranged from biographical anecdotes to topographical data to "modes of education, private or publick."

Belknap concluded the circular with this postscript: "Any books, pamphlets, manuscripts, maps or plans which may conduce to the accomplishment of the views of the Society; and any natural or artificial productions which may enlarge its museum, will be accepted with thanks." He also informed his correspondents that the Society would pay postage costs for all materials sent to it, no small inducement in that period.

It is not known how many circulars Belknap distributed in his six-year tenure as corresponding secretary. His letters reveal repeated references to the circular. Some insight into the extent of distribution can be gleaned from the Society action on January 27, 1795, of reprinting 1,000 copies of the document.[20] Certainly, every one with whom Belknap corresponded—and it was a lengthy list—received a copy. He scattered these documents far and wide. While he designed them for "every Gentleman of Science in the Continent and Islands of America," he also sent copies to a number of learned men in Great Britain and on the Continent and, in the judgment of one commentator, "to persons almost at the ends of the earth."[21]

Belknap utilized the "chain letter" technique to spread the word. He entreated recipients of the circular to pass it on to friends, corre-

---

19. The *American Apollo* is discussed below. The Society reprinted the "Circular Letter" of 1791 in 1966 to commemorate its 175th anniversary. An undated manuscript copy of the "Circular Letter" is in Records of Recording Secretary, 1791-1813, vol. 1.

20. Two other "Circular Letters" were produced before the 1794 edition. Internal evidence suggests runs of 500 each. A committee was assigned the task of developing the circular in 1794. Belknap, a member, wrote the text. He made a number of revisions from the earlier two issues. See Mass. Hist. Soc., *Procs.*, 1 (1791-1835): intro., xx-xxiv, 24n, 61, 67, 67n, 81.

21. George E. Ellis, "Jeremy Belknap," *Atlantic Monthly* 67 (1891): 654.

spondents, and any others who might be prospective donors. He also suggested that they have it printed in local newspapers.

Some readily acceded to his requests. David Ramsay, for example, sent the circular he received to both houses of the South Carolina legislature, which passed a resolution to donate to the Society "every official printed paper." He also had the notice printed in the *South-Carolina State-Gazette*, the state's largest and most influential paper. Alexander Spark of Quebec saw to it that the circular was printed in the *Quebec Magazine* both "in French and English."[22]

Belknap sought materials and historical information from residents of Boston who had been active participants in the American Revolution. The list included such prominent figures as John Hancock, Samuel Adams, and John Adams. He also badgered another Bostonian, "Colonel" Paul Revere, into writing an account of his nocturnal dash to Lexington on April 19, 1775, to alert the patriots on the coming of a British contingent. Belknap had informed Revere that his account would be deposited in the library. After receiving and reading the document, however, Belknap published it in 1798 in the Society's *Collections*.[23]

Belknap's attempt to secure congressional materials also reveals his aggressiveness as a collector.[24] On December 16, 1793, he joined forces with President Sullivan in a committee of two and petitioned the United States Congress for copies of "printed acts, journals, reports, treaties, letters, proceedings of courts-martial and other papers relative the the public affairs of the United States, civil and military, foreign and domestic." They directed the memorial to Congressman Peleg Coffin, a resident of Nantucket, who, not by coincidence, had been elected a member of the Society in August 1792.

A day after the memorial was sent to Coffin, Belknap dispatched

22. Ramsey to Belknap, Charleston, Mar. 2, 1795; Spark to Belknap, Quebec, Aug. 26, 1793, Correspondence of Corresponding Secretary, 1791-98, Massachusetts Historical Society Archives. Spark also sent Belknap a batch of reports.

23. "A Letter from Col. Paul Revere to the Corresponding Secretary," Mass. Hist. Soc., *Coll.*, 1st ser., 5:106-112. A slightly edited copy of the letter is printed in Mass. Hist. Soc., *Procs.*, 16 (1878): 371-376.

24. In addition to the letters contained in the Correspondence of Corresponding Secretary, 1791-98, see Belknap to Hazard, Boston, Dec. 20, 1793, Belknap Papers.

a personal letter to the congressman urging him to "enforce success to our application"—that is, he wanted Coffin personally to monitor the situation to make certain that positive action would ensue. As an afterthought, he asked Coffin to send along any other documents appropriate for the library.

Three years later, the Society elected Congressman Oliver Wolcott of Connecticut a corresponding member.[25] In short order, Wolcott received the predictable request from the ever-vigilant Belknap for important governmental documents not already possessed by the Society. Wolcott began to honor this request in 1797 and thereafter became a regular donor.[26]

Dogged persistence was Belknap's hallmark as a collector. After learning from President Ezra Stiles of Yale College that a Reverend Townsend of Barrington, Rhode Island, owned a body of manuscripts relating to the original settlers of New England, Belknap immediately wrote the minister and made a strong appeal for the documents. As was his custom, he inserted one of his circulars on the Society.

That same day, he wrote a letter to a Dr. Hitchcock of Providence in which he informed him of his communication to Townsend and enclosed a copy. If Townsend should send his documents to Hitchcock, wrote Belknap, he was to forward them to the Society. In an aside, Belknap inquired about the possibility of Hitchcock providing assistance in obtaining the papers of the late Gov. Samuel Hopkins of Rhode Island from his family. As usual, he enclosed a circular and requested Hitchcock to arrange for its publication in Rhode Island newspapers.

While Belknap was successful in extracting contributions from a number of European correspondents, he was especially fortunate when he befriended Christoph Daniel Ebeling of Hamburg, Germany.[27] The learned Ebeling, who referred to himself as a "cosmop-

25. Mass. Hist. Soc., *Procs.*, 1 (1791-1835): 102.

26. See *ibid.*, 111, 123, 130, 145.

27. For biographical data on Ebeling (1741-1817), see "Letters of Christoph Daniel Ebeling to Rev. Dr. William Bentley of Salem, Mass. and to other American Correspondents," ed. William Coolidge Lane, American Antiquarian Society, *Proceedings*, new ser., 35 (1925): 272-280; Michael Krause, *The Writing of American History* (Norman, Okla., 1953), 103-104.

olite," had taught Greek language and history at a gymnasium for many years; in the twilight of his career, he served as city librarian. His special interest as an historian was the New World, particularly the United States. He not only taught American history but also collected materials bearing upon the area and corresponded with a number of prominent American literati, including Ezra Stiles, Noah Webster, Jedidiah Morse, William Bentley, Timothy Pickering, David Ramsay, and Jeremy Belknap. In the process of preparing a history and geography of America, which took 20 years to complete, Ebeling amassed an enormous body of Americana, primarily newspapers, maps, and books. Like Belknap, he was also a fervent collector. He acquired many of these materials through exchanges with his American correspondents. Others he purchased at auctions in Germany. He acquired on publication most of the books printed contemporaneously in England and on the Continent relating to the New World. His collection of 18th-century American newspapers was one of the largest private holdings of the period. Despite his passion for America, he never visited the New World.

Belknap regarded his German colleague as a prime potential donor. As Chaucer wrote in *Troilus*, "to fisshen then he leyde out hooke and line." Belknap also laid out hook and line. His first step was to arrange for the election of Ebeling as a corresponding member, a strategy he frequently employed when courting prospective donors, both domestic and foreign.[28] Observing convention, Ebeling expressed elation at the "great honor" and then added some words which must have pleased his sponsor: "The honor I enjoy now shall be a great incitement to me to make myself worthy thereof as far as I may be able. I suppose the Society will not take it amiss that I have offered them some few maps lately published in Germany, and I take the liberty to join a few more." And Ebeling promised even more: "Some old books written in Latin in the 16 and 17 century

28. Mass. Hist. Soc., *Procs.*, 1 (1791-1835): 69, 77. Ebeling was elected in 1795. Belknap was his sponsor. Ebeling produced a 7-volume geographical work, *Erdbeschreibung und Geschichte von Amerika: Die Vereinten Staaten von Nordamerika* (Hamburg, 1793-1816). Daniel Boorstin has described it as "the first extensive and systematic geography of America." See Boorstin, *The Americans: The Colonial Experience* (New York, 1958), 160.

about America are occasionally to be found in auctions, and I shall be attentive to get them."[29]

Ebeling was a man of his word. He sent a steady stream of materials to his new friend in Boston, and Belknap reciprocated by forwarding copies of his *History of New Hampshire* and *American Biography*. But what the German scholar donated to the Society was only a small portion of his vast holdings of Americana. After his death, his residual collection was put up for sale. The purchaser was Col. Israel Thorndike of Boston, a merchant prince who had made a fortune in the China trade. He outbid the king of Prussia, bought the entire lot for $6,500, and then donated it to Harvard College. His gift made Harvard a leading center of Americana.

"Remember the ladies," the redoubtable Abigail Adams admonished her husband as John and his male colleagues formulated the Declaration of Independence that fateful summer of 1776 in Philadelphia.[30] Belknap made it a point to "remember the ladies" as he developed the library. While women were excluded by social tradition from membership in the Society at this time (there was no explicit exclusion in the constitution or bylaws), they were welcomed as contributors of materials and Belknap avidly solicited gifts from them.

In seeking to secure manuscripts from the Misses Mary ("Polly") and Catherine ("Kitty") Byles,[31] the elderly daughters of his great-uncle Mather Byles, he exuded the charm of a modern solicitor of gifts for charitable purposes. Writing to "My dear girls," he gently

29. Ebeling to Belknap, Hamburg, June 28, 1795, Mass. Hist. Soc., *Coll.,* 6th ser., 4:595-596. Ebeling sent Belknap two books written in German. Belknap did not read German, so he sent them to William Bentley of Salem and requested an "explanation" of their contents. See Belknap to Bentley, Boston, Aug. 21, 1795, Correspondence of Corresponding Secretary, 1791-98. Ebeling also sent Belknap a catalogue of his vast holdings on American history, a list of 3,000-3,500 titles, excluding his manuscripts and maps. The catalogue has disappeared from the Society's collections, unfortunately.

30. Abigail Adams to John Adams, Braintree, Mar. 31, 1776, Adams Papers.

31. Neither woman married and, like their father, both remained devout tories, keeping the king's birthday and drinking to his health. They decreed that all of their household possessions be shipped to Nova Scotia after their deaths. See Shipton, *Sibley's Harvard Graduates,* 7:489-490.

importuned: "Mr [George] Whitefield used to say that 'we should make the end of one good work the beginning of another.' You have done one good work in giving Burgess's Commission to the historical society and if you will give any or all of the parchments which I now return to you, to the same institution the gift will be cordially accepted."[32] Shortly after receiving the letter, the "dear girls" donated "Two very Curious Manuscripts in Parchment." Belknap inserted the names of the spinsters, as well as their donation, in his periodic listings of contributors in the *American Apollo* and rendered thanks to them in his prefatory statement.[33] Extant records reveal that seven women made contributions during Belknap's period as corresponding secretary.[34]

Perhaps more than any other officer, Belknap recognized the value of corresponding members as potential donors to the library. He worked assiduously to develop a network of such members across the nation and western Europe.[35]

An incident in 1795 illustrates Belknap's interest in acquiring corresponding members. St. George Tucker, a leading member of one of the First Families of Virginia and a professor of law at the College of William and Mary, had corresponded and exchanged publications with some of the Boston literati, including Belknap. The latter regarded Tucker as an ideal candidate for membership. The Society elected him on August 17, 1795, and Belknap routinely communicated the good news.[36]

To Belknap's surprise and consternation, the prominent Virginian declined the invitation. His stated reason was, as Belknap phrased it: "It seems to be your idea that none but men of *fortune and leisure* can attend to the researches necessary to carry our design into execution."

32. Belknap to Miss Polly and Miss Kitty Byles, Boston, Apr. 25, 1793, Belknap Papers.

33. May 3, 1793.

34. Based upon an examination of Belknap's lists in the *American Apollo*.

35. In 1798, there were corresponding members in ten states, Halifax, Quebec, Edinburgh, London, Hamburg, Ireland, and Bavaria.

36. Mass. Hist. Soc., *Procs.*, 1 (1791-1835): 86-87.

"If that were true," Belknap responded, "we must all resign. There is not *one* Person among us who answers to the description. All excepting 3 or 4 Bachelors have families to support and are obliged to use constant exertions for that purpose. But still the business of the Society is carried on." He assured Tucker that the Society only wished that every member, resident and corresponding, "would *feel interested* in promoting our views and *do what he can* consistently with his other Engagements to do it. If whether at home or abroad you feel this disposition and whenever an opportunity presents, make such observations or procure such documents as may serve the general design, it will be fully complying with our Expectations."

Belknap pleaded with Tucker "as a private friend" to reconsider his decision, informing him that he would not submit his letter of declination to the Society until he had received his response. And he concluded his epistle with this salient point: "How different are the dispositions of men! Some are wishing and seeking for admission into our Society, but we will not admit them because We conceive that they aim only at a feather in their Cap, and would be but drones in the hive. Others are men of genius and merit with whom we wish to associate and they decline!"[37]

Belknap's remonstration was successful. Tucker agreed to become a corresponding member and remained so until his death in 1828. Society records reveal that he made two contributions to the library.[38]

If Belknap occasionally experienced difficulties in acquiring corresponding members, he also faced problems periodically in collecting documents. The acquisition of the correspondence of William Samuel Johnson in 1795 is a case in point.

In 1770 the General Assembly of Connecticut began to show concern over the loss of the colony's public papers and took steps to recover them. In its May 1771 session, the Assembly resolved that Gov. Jonathan Trumbull should "collect all publick letters and pa-

37. See Tucker to Belknap, Williamsburg, Oct. 31, 1795, Mass. Hist. Soc., *Coll.*, 5th ser., 3:416-417; Tucker to Belknap, Nov. 27, 1795, *ibid.*, 422-423; Belknap to Tucker, Boston, Dec. 28, 1795, Belknap Papers.

38. See Mass. Hist. Soc., *Procs.*, 1 (1791-1835): 98, 112. He also maintained a vibrant correspondence with Belknap on public issues, like the slavery problem.

pers which may hereafter in any way affect the interest of this
Colony and have the same bound together, that they may be preserved."[39]

An avid historian, Trumbull took this charge seriously and collected a large amount of materials: agents' letters, 1742-1773; council of safety papers, 1775-1782; council orders, 1743-1775; Gov.
Joseph Talcott's papers, 1724-1741; Gov. Jonathan Law's papers,
1741-1750; and Gov. Thomas Fitch's papers, 1754-1766. In sum,
these materials constituted the extant collection on the political history of the colony. In the tradition of the times, Trumbull carted the
collection to his home in Lebanon when he left office. When he died
in 1785, the documents became part of his estate.

In April 1794, David Trumbull, the son of the deceased governor,
sent Belknap the type of letter the corresponding secretary welcomed. Writing from the ancestral home in Lebanon, Trumbull informed Belknap that his father had "collected with care, the most
important official papers which pass'd thro his hands, during the
very interesting Period of the Revolution, with the intention that
they should be preserv'd and deposited in some public Library, as
materials for future Historians."

"Had the Massachusetts Historical Society existed during his
Life," continued David, "there is no doubt but He would have
chosen to give them to an Institution whose Patriotic Views they
would so directly subserve in preference to a Collegiate or other Library, where they probably would soon become 'Food for Worms.'"

And then, the critical conclusion: "His heirs therefore, think they
cannot so well fulfill the Governor's intentions on this subject, as
by Offering them, as I am commissioned to do—to the Massachusetts Historical Society."[40]

Belknap took the perfunctory step of informing the Society of
Trumbull's generous offer. The body quickly voted to accept the gift
and directed Belknap to notify the donors that a "suitable person

39. Quoted in Christopher P. Bickford, "Public Records and the Private Historical Society: A Connecticut Example," *Government Publications Review*, 8A
(1981): 314.

40. Trumbull to Belknap, Lebanon, Conn., Apr. 15, 1794, Correspondence of
Corresponding Secretary 1791-98; the letter is printed in Mass. Hist. Soc., *Coll.*,
4th ser., 2:240.

will be sent to Connecticut as soon as possible to make a selection."[41] In his letter, Belknap thanked Trumbull and informed him that he was unable to travel to Lebanon to arrange for the transportation of the papers to Boston but would send an agent in his stead. He then added a standard request: "Should there be among your printed pamphlets any Election or Funeral discourses or other matters" which would be of value to the Society, he should add them "to the parcel."[42]

Belknap arranged to have William Wetmore, a fellow member, undertake this mission. Belknap carefully instructed Wetmore: "I need not remind you that we wish for as large a collection as possible; and that the transportation be as little expensive as may consist with the safety of the Parcel."[43] That is, take as much as you can, but keep the shipping costs down.

For unknown reasons, Wetmore was unable to carry out the assignment. Belknap himself made the "excursion" the following summer. Traveling on the mail stage by way of Providence, Rhode Island, and Norwich, Connecticut, he arrived in Lebanon on July 9; it was a grueling, two-day journey for a man not in the best of health. He spent the next four days processing and packing papers and arranging for their shipment to Boston.[44]

On July 30, Belknap reported to the Society on his successful mission and submitted his expense account amounting to $17.19.[45] Previously, the Society had voted to reimburse him for one-half of his expenses.[46] After a circuitous voyage, "the chests and boxes of papers" arrived at Belknap's home on December 12. They had traveled from Lebanon to Norwich, from there to Barnstable on Cape Cod, then to Boston by ship.[47]

41. Mass. Hist. Soc., *Procs.*, 1 (1791-1835): 68.

42. Belknap to Trumbull, June 12, 1794, Letterbook, Massachusetts Historical Society Archives.

43. Belknap to Wetmore, June 11, 1794, Letterbook, Massachusetts Historical Society Archives.

44. Diary, see entries for July 1795; Belknap to Hazard, Boston, Aug. 21, 1795, Mass. Hist. Soc., *Coll.*, 5th ser., 3: 356.

45. Mass. Hist. Soc., *Procs.*, 1 (1791-1835): 85.

46. *Ibid.*, 83.

47. Diary, Dec. 12, 1795.

By any standard, the Trumbull collection was a remarkable acquisition. It included files on the Susquehanna and Pequot Indian land disputes; military affairs during the Revolution; Trumbull's correspondence with generals George Washington, Philip Schuyler, Horatio Gates, and John Sullivan, and Gov. William Tryon, presidents of Congress, and Connecticut delegates to Congress; and copies of the correspondence of governors Fitch and Pitkin with British secretaries of state.[48]

Also included in the Trumbull treasure trove were volumes one and two of Gov. John Winthrop's three-volume, manuscript "Journal of John Winthrop," alternatively known as "the History of New England"—and therein lies a tale.

When Governor Winthrop died in 1649, his magisterial document on the history of Massachusetts Bay Colony from 1630 to 1649 devolved to his heirs. Thereafter, leading members of the family in turn assumed custody of the manuscript. The Winthrops willingly lent the "Journal" to those historians who requested it. Nathaniel Morton used it in the 1660s when he was writing his *New England's Memorial*. William Hubbard of Ipswich borrowed it when he wrote his *General History of New England*.[49] And Cotton Mather did likewise when he undertook his *Magnalia Christi Americana*. These authors returned all three volumes. About 1755, Thomas Prince, who was in the process of compiling his *Annals of New England*, borrowed the manuscript from John Still Winthrop. This historical squirrel returned only the first two parts, which covered the period 1630-1644. He retained the third segment. It is not known if Winthrop gave him permission to do so.

As time passed, everyone (including the Winthrops) apparently forgot the third volume, and it came to be thought that the two remaining volumes constituted the entire "Journal." In 1771, Ezra Stiles, then residing in Newport, Rhode Island, borrowed the work

48. See the report of the Committee charged with the responsibility of cataloguing the Society's manuscripts, including the Trumbull Collection. Mass. Hist. Soc., *Procs.*, 2nd ser., 4 (1887-1889): 103-105. The Committee members were Justin Winsor and Robert C. Winthrop, Jr. They submitted their report in 1888.

49. Hubbard completed his manuscript in the late 17th century. While the document was used by a number of later historians, it was not published until 1815. It first appeared in Mass. Hist. Soc., *Coll.*, 2nd ser., vols. 5-6.

while he was preparing his "Ecclesiastical History of New England," one of the many writing projects he never completed.[50] He dutifully returned it.

The next borrower was Gov. Jonathan Trumbull. He acquired the "Journal" at the start of the American Revolution. He intended to edit and publish it. His death in 1785 brought an end to the project.[51] The "Journal" came to rest in the Trumbull ancestral home with the other historical materials collected by the governor. Trumbull's heirs were perhaps unaware that the "Journal" had been borrowed. The Winthrops, moreover, may have forgotten they had lent it since they did not press for its return.

Enter Jeremy Belknap. He had learned from Hazard in 1781 that Trumbull had borrowed the "Journal."[52] He was fully aware of Trumbull's plan to edit and publish it. So it must not have come as a surprise when he discovered the two fragile, vellum-covered notebooks among the governor's holdings in Lebanon. Belknap's subsequent action was predictable. He packed them for shipment to Boston. There is no evidence that he sought, or was given, permission to do so.[53]

50. Edmund S. Morgan, *The Gentle Puritan: A Life of Ezra Stiles* (New Haven, London, 1962), ch 9. (titled "A Library of Unfinished Books").

51. There were others interested in publishing the "Journal." Hazard, Jedidiah Morse, and even Belknap gave it serious thought. Noah Webster carried it beyond the thinking stage and published an edition in Hartford in 1790.

52. Webster sought to involve Belknap in his project as an editorial advisor. He sent him a copy of his manuscript and added: "Should it be published, I could wish you to superintend the business, omit any improper passages, make out a table or index, etc." See Webster to Belknap, Boston, May 7, 1789, Mass. Hist. Soc., *Coll.*, 6th ser., 4:430. Belknap rejected the offer, claiming he lacked the time.

53. Some curious developments took place when the "Journal" reached Boston. All is not known, but this we do know. When Belknap died, the two volumes were in his home, not in the Society's library, and they were incorporated into his estate. This raises some interesting questions. Did he deposit the "Journal" in the library with the remainder of the Trumbull materials and later borrow it for personal use? Or did he remove it from the main corpus before delivering the collection to the library? There is no evidence that he notified the Winthrops that he had taken the "Journal" from Trumbull's home and shipped it to Boston.

At the turn of the 19th century, Thomas Lindall Winthrop, a resident of Boston and member of the Society, began a search for the manuscript. He learned that the Belknap family had it. He asked for its return and Belknap's

Belknap did not take the entire collection at Lebanon. He left behind a large body of equally significant materials: agents' letters, 1742-1773; council of safety papers, 1775-1782; council orders, 1743-1775; Gov. Joseph Talcott's papers, 1724-1741; Gov. Jonathan Law's papers, 1741-1750; and Gov. Thomas Fitch's papers, 1754-1766.[54]

Why Belknap did not take the entire collection, as was his practice on other occasions, is a mystery. Given his acquisitive spirit, it is highly unlikely that he did not covet all these items. His correspondence with David Trumbull does not suggest any restrictions or limitations on what he could take. There are intimations that he was free to take more than the governor's papers.

Writing in 1981, Christopher P. Bickford, director of the Connecticut Historical Society, theorized that the Trumbulls developed second thoughts on what Belknap should cart off after he arrived at Lebanon; that they made a distinction between one segment of the collection, which they were inclined to view as "private" holdings and therefore disposable, and the remainder which bore the character of "public" documents and were not the property of the family.[55]

heirs willingly complied with his request. In 1803, Winthrop donated the two volumes to the Society in behalf of their legal owner, Francis Bayard Winthrop. In 1816, the third volume was discovered in the Old South tower. It was "buried beneath a mass of pamphlets and papers" in Prince's collection. It, too, was donated to the Society. In 1825, the Society's librarian, James Savage, a lawyer who was preparing a new edition of the "Journal," borrowed the second volume. A fire destroyed his law office and the treasured volume.

On the matters noted above, see: Mass. Hist. Soc., *Procs.*, 2nd ser., 8 (1892-1894): 139-141; *ibid.*, 12 (1871-1873): 233-236; Malcolm Freiberg, "The Winthrops and Their Papers," *ibid.*, 80 (1968): 55-70; Hazard to Belknap, Jamaica Plain, Sept. 5, 1781, Mass. Hist. Soc., *Coll.*, 5th ser., 2:106; *ibid.*, 7th ser., 3:xiv-xvi; *ibid.*, 2nd ser., 4:200-202; *Winthrop Papers, 1498-1628* (Boston, 1929), 1: preface, v-viii; Richard S. Dunn, "John Winthrop Writes His Journal," *William and Mary Quarterly*, 3rd ser., 41 (1984): 185-188; John Winthrop, *The History of New England from 1630 to 1649*, ed. James Savage, 2 vols. (Boston, 1853), 1: preface, vii; Emily Ellsworth Fowler Ford, comp., and Emily Ellsworth Ford Skeel, ed., *Notes on the Life of Noah Webster*, 2 vols. (New York, 1912), 1:288, 300-303.

54. The residue of the collection was deposited in the Connecticut Historical Society in 1840. See Bickford, "Public Records and the Private Historical Society," 8A (1981): 313-315.

55. *Ibid.*, 315.

As things turned out, Belknap may have been grateful that he did not acquire the entire collection. One segment alone soon became an albatross. But Belknap himself was responsible for provoking the difficulty. His passion for "multiplying the copies" was the source of the problem.

While sorting and packing the materials in Lebanon, Belknap discovered a bound volume of William Samuel Johnson's correspondence with governors William Pitkin and Trumbull covering the years 1767-1771. Johnson had written the letters while he was serving as Connecticut colonial agent in London.

The son of Samuel Johnson, the noted Anglican churchman and first president of King's College, William was a prominent figure in his own right.[56] A graduate of Yale College (like his father), he had distinguished himself in law, diplomacy, and politics and was one of the state's brightest lights. He had served in the Continental Congress, represented Connecticut at the Constitutional Convention of 1787, and held office as a United States senator. Following in the footsteps of his father, he became president of King's College in 1787 and served in that prestigious position until 1800.

Belknap was excited by his find. As he later wrote: "I have read them repeatedly with delight; and have gained a better Idea of the political system, than from all the Books published during that period."[57] So taken was he by the letters that he carried the volume with him on the stage and read them on the bumpy ride back to Boston. Realizing that the documents were of significant historical value, he decided to give the public a "rich repast" of them—that is, he would publish a selection in the Society's *Collections*.[58]

56. On William Samuel Johnson, see G. C. Groce, Jr., *William Samuel Johnson* (New York, 1937); Elizabeth P. McCaughey, *From Loyalist to Founding Father: The Political Odyssey of William Samuel Johnson* (New York, 1980); E. Edwards Beardsley, *Life and Times of William Samuel Johnson, First Senator in Congress From Connecticut and President of Columbia College, New York*, 2nd ed. (New York and Boston, 1886).

57. Quoted in a letter from Jonathan Trumbull, Jr., to W. S. Johnson, Philadelphia, Feb. 2, 1796, in Oscar Zeichner, ed., "Jeremy B——p and the William Samuel Johnson Correspondence," *New England Quarterly*, 14 (1941): 373.

58. Belknap to Ebenezer Hazard, Boston, Aug. 21, 1795, Mass. Hist. Soc., *Coll.*, 5th ser., 3: 356.

As a courtesy, Belknap sent a perfunctory letter to Johnson, requesting his permission to print the correspondence. It was apparent that he did not anticipate a negative response. After making his request, he appended the usual appeal for additional documents: "whether it be in your power to contribute anything further to aid the cause in which we are engaged."[59]

To Belknap's surprise and dismay, Johnson denied his request. In the stilted phrasing of E. Edwards Beardsley, an early biographer, Johnson made "a strenuous and somewhat indignant remonstrance."[60] Indeed, he was violently incensed and his response barely concealed his rage. He affirmed that his letters "were generally written in much haste" and were not intended for publication. "They must therefore unavoidably contain many trifling articles of intelligence, many insignificant remarks, many crude observations, must in a word be in all respects extremely incorrect and totally unfit for the public eye." Their publication, he continued, would not only be an *"irreperable injury to me* but an *insult to the public."* Johnson demanded that Belknap return the manuscripts either to himself or to the Trumbull family. As for Belknap's request for additional documents, it was possible, he wrote, that he had "some things proper to the purposes of the Society; but I am *so anxious* that I can at present think of *nothing else."*[61] Belknap was assuredly perceptive enough to grasp the veiled threat; he would receive absolutely nothing unless the documents were returned.

That same day, Johnson fired off a salvo to Jonathan Trumbull, Jr., another son of the late governor, then serving as a United States senator. He excoriated the Trumbull family for donating his correspondence to the Society and accused them of violating private friendship and public trust. He had sent many letters to Gov. Trumbull while he was in England, wrote Johnson. Some were of a personal nature, some were official documents. In his view, the Trum-

59. Belknap to Johnson, Boston, Nov. 7, 1795, *ibid.*, 5th ser., 9:xii-xiii.

60. Beardsley, *Johnson*, 149.

61. Johnson to Belknap, New York, Dec. 15, 1795, quoted in Zeichner, "Belknap and Johnson Correspondence," *New England Quarterly*, 14 (1941): 367-368. The key correspondence of the controversy that followed is printed on 363-374. See also "Report on the Trumbull Papers," Mass. Hist. Soc., *Coll.*, 5th ser., 9:vii-xv; and Beardsley, *Johnson*, 213-219.

bulls should have retained all of the private letters. As for the public documents, if the family wished to dispose of them, they were legally obligated to place them in the custody of Connecticut's secretary of state. They rightfully belonged in the state's archives. Under no circumstances should any of the letters have been given to the Massachusetts Historical Society, Johnson contended.[62]

After receiving Johnson's stern document, Belknap sent copies of his original letter and his adversary's bristling reply to Jonathan Trumbull, Jr., and requested advice on the course of action he should take. While soliciting advice, he forcefully asserted the right of the Trumbulls to donate the correspondence to the Society and the right of the Society to accept them: "The Letters which we wished and asked his permission to publish were doubtless the *property* of Governor Trumbull and by him destined as materials for a part of American History. The *property* has been fairly transferred to our Society and I do not see any reason that Dr. Johnson has to expect that we will *return* them to him. . . . There is nothing in them that can 'injure his Character' much less 'insult the public' and why his indignation should be raised to such a degree is beyond my power to conjecture. His letters are not in the hands of 'mercenary booksellers nor avowed enemies' and had he expressed his disapprobation of our wish in terms *less energetic* he would have answered his purpose full as well and have saved me and you the trouble and disgust which we must feel from the perusing his Letter."[63]

The Trumbulls were now caught in a withering cross fire. Seeking to defuse the controversy, Jonathan composed a restrained response to Johnson. He explained the background of the gift and the family's motivation in making it. They acted "upon the principle of their [the manuscripts] being placed in a situation better adapted to their preservation—and more open to observation and use by any future historian, who might have occasion to consult original documents."

He had seen Belknap after the documents were transferred to Boston, Trumbull continued, and had mentioned to him that there was a possibility that some of the letters might be of "private family

62. Zeichner, "Belknap and Johnson Correspondence," *New England Quarterly*, 14 (1941): 364-365.

63. Belknap to Trumbull, Boston, Dec. 26, 1795, quoted in *ibid.*, 369-370.

Nature—and some others perhaps which properly belonged to the office of the Secretary of the State—and thereupon gave him my particular request and desire, that if he found any such, he would carefully select them from the general mass—and, that they might be returned where due—to this the Doctor consented—and promised to pay attention to my Caution—since this conversation, I have not seen him or heard from him." Trumbull was certain that Belknap would not "suffer them to be printed."[64]

Johnson was not placated by Trumbull's letter. He continued to seethe. The dispute increased in intensity and provoked more correspondence among the aggrieved parties.

In January 1796, Belknap became "very sick" and requested John Eliot to take up his cause. Perhaps reflecting a change in Belknap's attitude, Eliot struck a more conciliatory pose. He informed Jonathan Trumbull, Jr., that the Society "have no idea of publishing" the letters, if Johnson was so adamant on the issue. But he adjured Trumbull to allow the Society to keep them as a "choice treasure": "they shall have a place in the most retired apartments of our Cabinet or among the papers of the Corresponding Secretary, where it will not be in any one's power to make a 'bad use of them.' If the light must be hid let it not be extinguished. We should be guilty of a breach of trust in our official characters as members of the H. Society should we suffer these valuable Mss to be lost."[65]

A relieved Trumbull informed Johnson of the Society's decision and the acrimonious dispute came to an end.[66] In a final communication to Trumbull, Belknap wrote: "I hope the old Gentleman's violent sensibilities are before this Time allayed by the soothing dose which you have administered, which I think supersedes the necessity of my writing to him."[67] Johnson abandoned his effort to retrieve the manuscripts and they remained with the Society. Nor did the Trumbulls request their return.[68]

64. Trumbull to Johnson, Philadelphia, Dec. 22, 1795, quoted in *ibid.*, 366-367.

65. Eliot to Trumbull, Boston, Jan. 16, 1796, quoted in *ibid.*, 371-372.

66. Trumbull to Johnson, Philadelphia, Feb. 3, 1796, quoted in *ibid.*, 373.

67. Belknap to Trumbull, Boston, Feb. 13, 1796, quoted in *ibid.*, 374.

68. The State of Connecticut did, however, starting in 1845. Connecticut officials affirmed that the entire collection represented public papers and properly belonged in the office of Secretary of State. They threatened legal action. The

Why was Johnson so adamantly opposed to Belknap's plan to publish his correspondence? Should we accept the reasons he offered to Belknap as his sole concerns? A recent biographer of Johnson has presented another, and more plausible, explanation for his position: his past record as a loyalist during the Revolution.[69]

While in England as Connecticut's colonial agent, Johnson developed a warm sympathy for the Crown's position in the growing dispute with the colonies. This did not endear him to the "patriots" in the Land of Steady Habits. When the rupture finally occurred, he became a passive loyalist and dropped out of public life. It was an expedient course of action since he was not a popular figure in Whig-dominated Connecticut. By refusing to swear allegiance to the Oath of Fidelity Act, which was passed in 1777, he was forced to abandon his lucrative law practice. He paid a high price for dissent: financial hardship and social isolation.

After the Revolution, Johnson reentered the public arena. Through his dedicated and constructive public service, he was able to rehabilitate his tarnished reputation and erase the stigma of his loyalist past.

When Belknap made his request to Johnson in 1795, the United States and Great Britain had just signed the Jay Treaty, which provoked a bitter dispute in the young nation. A wave of Anglophobia swept across America. Johnson was troubled by a revival of Anglo-American tension. Was he fearful that the publication of his letters would place a spotlight on his tainted past and once again arouse the hostility of his American compatriots? In his old age, would he be forced to do battle once more on the issue of his loyalty to America? Would his historical reputation suffer in the process? Johnson made no mention of the loyalist issue in his correspondence with

Society rejected Connecticut's claim to the documents. Periodically, during the next 65 years, Connecticut renewed its demand, but the Society stood firm. Finally, in 1921, the Society considered the matter again and decided to relent. The formal transfer to the newly developed Connecticut State Library took place on Sept. 17, 1921, in Hartford. Society President (and U.S. Senator) Henry Cabot Lodge, Worthington C. Ford, and Arthur Lord represented the Boston institution. Gov. Everett J. Lake of Connecticut sponsored, and presided over, an elegant luncheon at a private club. A formal program in Memorial Hall followed this festive occasion. See "Return of the Trumbull Papers," Mass. Hist. Soc., Procs., 55 (1921-1922): 30-40.

69. See McCaughey, Johnson, 266-267.

Belknap or the Trumbulls, but it may provide an answer for the intensity of his opposition.

On the surface, the Belknap-Johnson-Trumbull imbroglio would appear to have been another of the interminable personal, parochial squabbles of the period. But, as Professor Oscar Zeichner has shown, this was a significant episode in American history. Vital principles were at issue. If not the "first," it was the earliest recorded example of an American historian being confronted with a demand that he not publish primary source material. Similarly, if not the "first," it was the earliest recorded case of a learned society experiencing difficulties in using the personal papers of a living historical figure. While he was forced to capitulate on the issue of publication, Belknap achieved a partial victory by managing to retain ownership of the documents for the Society. Ninety years later, his cause was vindicated when the Society published Johnson's correspondence.[70]

How successful was Belknap as a collector? For this era, he was without parallel in the United States. His was a singular achievement. He was the master builder of the Society's library which became the cornerstone of the new organization.

The *American Apollo* became an important element in Belknap's plan to lay a firm foundation for the Society.[71] In the fall of 1791, Belknap's oldest son, 22-year-old Joseph, who had been trained as a printer, joined forces with another Bostonian, Alexander Young, and established a printing firm. The two men decided to publish a weekly periodical, a common course of action for printers at the time.

It may have been more than felicitous coincidence that Jeremy Belknap was profoundly interested in this project. He knew that a

70. Mass. Hist. Soc., *Coll.*, 5th ser., 9:211-490. The editorial note on vii-xiv presents the background on Belknap's acquisition of the Trumbull collection and contains key letters from Belknap, Johnson, and Trumbull pertaining to the controversy.

71. The prime sources for the Society's involvement with the *American Apollo* program are: minutes of Society meetings in Records of Recording Secretary, 1791-1813; printed extracts of Society business meetings in Mass. Hist. Soc., *Procs.*, 1 (1791-1835): *passim* (there is a chronological account of this relationship in the introduction of this volume, xxiv-xxxiii); and Correspondence of Corresponding Secretary, 1791-1813.

periodical could be used to great advantage in strengthening the Society. One is thus led to wonder if he inspired his son to undertake
this venture.

Initially, there was Belknap's concern about preserving sources
for future historians, his primary reason for founding the historical
society. He was well aware that establishing a library provided no
assurance that a collection would survive for all time. Libraries were
vulnerable to fires, natural disasters, vandalism, and other perils and
could be destroyed quickly. A recent reminder was the catastrophic
Harvard library fire of 1764, when the entire collection was con-
sumed in a brilliant inferno. By printing documents in thousands
of copies, Belknap believed he could solve the problem of saving
sources. Whatever disasters befell the Society, whether man-made
or acts of God, some copies were bound to survive.

Belknap was also motivated by a practical concern which involved
contemporary researchers. He knew that few, if any, American historians could afford the expense or time to travel to one city, much
less the entire nation, to conduct research. In his view, distributing
sources through publication was a sensible expedient.

Belknap also sensed that the proposed periodical was an ideal
vehicle for communicating historical information to the general public "in a literary way." This fit in with his conviction that the Society
should seek to educate the masses about American history, thereby
promoting public virtue and patriotism.

Belknap foresaw still a fourth advantage in having access to a
publication. He could use this vehicle to solicit donations for the
library and promote Society activities, as, for example, its publications and public lectures. It was an excellent "public relations" tool,
a far more effective instrument for spreading the word than the
circular.

There was perhaps also a personal motive in Belknap's desire to
link the Society with his son's newspaper. As a parent, he was naturally concerned about the financial well-being of his son "Josey"
and anxious to assist him in his first business enterprise. There was
ample cause for his concern. He knew that Joseph was destined for
the life of a tradesman.

In the normal course of events in 18th-century New England, Jo-

seph would have been educated at Harvard and followed in his
father's footsteps. This was the common path for the eldest son of
a Harvard-trained minister. A first son enjoyed preferential attention. But Joseph lacked sufficient education to qualify for admission
to Harvard.

Since Dover was without a public school during the period of
Belknap's residence, and because he did not have the financial means
to send Joseph or his other children away to school, he was forced
to function as a teacher. He was not especially successful in this
endeavor and was deeply remorseful for his failure to provide his
children with a proper education. As he informed Hazard, it was "a
subject of contemplation which has employed many melancholy
hours for several years past."[72] Some of his sharpest criticism of
the Dover citizenry centered on their failure to establish a public
school. He deemed it unconscionable that they steadfastly refused
to appropriate funds for even a temporary "scholar," that is, a
schoolteacher.

Belknap especially despaired Joseph's "want of education." His
only recourse was to arrange for the youth's training as a tradesman.
If his son were to achieve financial security in his life, it would have
to be in the business world. With Hazard's assistance, Belknap arranged to have Joseph serve as an apprentice to Robert Aiken, a
Philadelphia printer. Joseph began his apprenticeship in 1785. Less
than two years later, it ended because of Aiken's habit of using the
"fist" and "knotted cord" in administering discipline.[73] Joseph returned home and in 1789 began a second apprenticeship with John
Mycall of Newburyport. Two years later, he was sufficiently trained
to open his own printing shop in Boston.

This fortunate conjunction of interests and objectives led to the
formation of a business relationship between the Society and the
firm of Belknap and Young. At the Society meeting of October 11,
1791, Jeremy presented a proposal from his son's firm "for a new
periodical publication which they propose to carry on (with the as-

72. Belknap to Hazard, Dover, Dec. 21, 1783, Mass. Hist. Soc., *Coll.*, 5th ser.,
2:287. In this letter, Belknap vented his spleen against the Dover citizenry for
their failure to establish a public school.

73. Joseph's apprenticeship was a principal topic of discussion in the Bel-
knap-Hazard correspondence during this period. See *ibid.*, *passim.*

sistance of the Historical Society), under the title of the *American Apollo*." The Society approved the plan and appointed a committee to meet with the printers and work out a formal agreement.[74] Possibly to avoid a conflict of interest, the members did not appoint Jeremy to this committee; while no mention is made in the Society's minutes, it is conceivable that Jeremy voluntarily begged off from the assignment because of the sensitive nature of the relationship.

The meeting took place and an agreement was concluded on October 24, 1791. The printers agreed to add to each issue a four- or eight-page supplement which would be stitched into the same covers and contain material the Society provided. The Society was to be wholly responsible for the contents of the historical segment. In addition, the printers agreed to supply the Society with 50 complimentary copies of the supplement.[75] The printers would assume the major cost of the project. It was, in effect, a "risk" venture for the firm.

Belknap and Young issued a printed proposal of the paper in an effort to enroll subscribers. They set the price at $2 per year, with 50 cents to be paid in advance. The Society and its projected publications received top billing in the prospectus. Even the ten members were listed.[76]

The *American Apollo* made its debut on January 6, 1792, almost a year after the Society's founding.[77] Presented in octavo form, it was printed on the "first complete Printing-Press ever made in this town."[78] Jeremy affixed an "introductory address" to the historical segment in which he explained the purpose of the publication.

The American people, Belknap began, enjoyed the great advantage of being able to trace the history of their nation to its founding.

74. Minutes of Oct. 11, 1791, meeting, Records of Recording Secretary, 1791-1813; Mass. Hist. Soc., *Procs.*, 1 (1791-1835): 16-17.

75. Minutes of Oct. 24 meeting, Records of Recording Secretary, 1791-1813; Mass. Hist. Soc., *Procs.*, 1 (1791-1835): 23.

76. *Proposal of Joseph Belknap and Alexander Young, For Printing a Weekly Paper; to be Entitled The American Apollo* . . . (Boston, 1791).

77. The Society has a complete set of this newspaper. For the history of the paper, see Clarence S. Brigham, *History and Bibliography of American Newspapers, 1690-1820*, 2 vols. (Worcester, 1947), 1: 271.

78. *American Apollo*, Jan. 6, 1792.

They were able "to ascertain with precision many circumstances, the knowledge of which must have been either disfigured or lost among a people rude and unlettered." Given such an advantage, Belknap continued, it would be wholly inexcusable if Americans neglected "to preserve authentic monuments of every memorable occurrence. Not only names, dates and facts may be thus handed down to posterity; but principles and reasonings, causes and consequences, with the manner of their operation and their various connexions, may enter into the mass of historical information."

He next noted the powerful historical impulse of New England's Puritan founding fathers which resulted in such seminal works as Gov. John Winthrop's "Journal," and William Hubbard's *General History of New England*. He cited Thomas Prince's numerous historical contributions, both as an author and collector.

Then he set forth one of his favorite themes. In the course of time, much valuable historical material had been lost or destroyed. He listed the more conspicuous examples, from Prince's collections to the Hutchinson documents to the Harvard College fire in 1764. It was a familiar litany of cultural woe. This led to his conclusion and ultimate solution: that "there is no sure way of preserving historical records and materials, but by *multiplying the copies*. The art of printing affords a mode of preservation more effectual than Corinthian brass or Egyptian marble; for statues and pyramids which have long survived the wreck of time, are unable to tell the names of their sculptors, or the date of their foundations."

The Historical Society, affirmed Belknap, was determined not only to collect but to "*diffuse* the various species of historical information" within its reach. It planned to publish documents as they were acquired. These would include a potpourri of information, not a chronologically consistent set of manuscripts. The Society was well aware of the limitations of this format, he wrote, but did not view it as a fatal flaw. "They [the Historical Society] cannot promise to erect a regular building; but they will plant a forest, into which every inquirer may enter at his pleasure, and find something suitable to his purpose."

The Society's first offering, Belknap announced, was a set of documents relating to the expedition to Cape Breton in 1745, "one of the most remarkable events in the history of this country." If one of Belknap's principal objectives was to promote patriotism and pride in Massachusetts' history, he could not have selected a more appropriate event to document, since the capture of Louisburg, the "Gibraltar of the New World," was to 18th-century New Englanders what the defeat of the Spanish Armada was to 16th-century Englishmen. Excluding the battles of Lexington and Concord, the defeat of the hated French in June 1745 was the most glorious military triumph in New England's history. The ground force that captured the mighty French fortress, one of the most powerful bastions in the New World, was composed almost entirely of Massachusetts troops. Moreover, the victory had been achieved with no assistance from Great Britain.

Because of the "novel and interesting" format, as well as Jeremy's intensive efforts in publicizing the project, the paper was a surprising success at the outset. Nearly 1,200 Bostonians signed on as subscribers. Jeremy alone managed the historical supplement. He selected the material and prepared copy for the printer.

The paper's success, however, was short-lived. Before the end of the second quarter, there was a sharp decline in subscriptions. Over 600 failed to renew. Joseph attributed the dramatic dip to "an almost universal misconstruction of the proposal." Notwithstanding Jeremy's opening statement in which he explained the proposed contents, the public expected a "regular history of America," not a random assortment of documents. This type of information, in Joseph's view, could not sustain the interest of the populace. After publishing 39 numbers between January 6 and September 28, 1792, which totaled 208 pages, Belknap and Young informed the Society that it could no longer afford to print the "papers of the Society" in the usual manner. They were losing money on the project. They therefore decided to enlarge the *Apollo* from an octavo to regular newspaper size and publish the historical segment separately on a monthly basis.[79]

79. Joseph Belknap to "The Committee of the Historical Society who contract printing," no date [late 1794? early 1795?], Records of the Recording Secretary, Massachusetts Historical Society Archives; Mass. Hist. Soc., *Procs.*, 1 (1791-1835): 42-43. The printers announced these changes in format to the subscribers in the *American Apollo*, Sept. 21, 1792.

This change in format provoked two special meetings of the Society in September at which the members pondered the problem and possible solutions. What emerged was predictable: the appointment of a special committee to analyze the issue in depth and submit a recommendation. Jeremy headed the list of committee members.[80]

A new arrangement resulted from these deliberations whereby the historical segment was published as a separate on a monthly basis with the Society agreeing to purchase 50 copies outright and all unsold copies, after a specified period, at the same price.[81] The monthly segments appeared in September, October, November, and December.

At the completion of the first year of publication, the Society decided to combine the 39 numbers issued between January and September, which totaled 208 pages, with the four monthly supplements, another 80 pages, and produce a volume of documents. This marked the beginning of the Society's *Collections* series which, in time, became a major source of American documentary history. The series was Belknap's brainchild; he inspired it, and he selected and edited the pieces that appeared therein.

The newspaper publication program limped on through 1793 and 1794. Public apathy persisted. Subscriptions continued to dwindle.

It was not an easy time for either participant in the joint venture. The Society began experiencing difficulties with the printers and charged them with "incorrectness" in their work. The printers pleaded "extenuating circumstances" and continued to suffer a financial loss, which led to bitter internal strife. Perhaps out of loyalty to his father, Joseph persisted in the relationship with the Society, notwithstanding the money he was losing. He finally split with Young over the financial issue, bought out his partner's interest, and took on another partner, Thomas Hall. "Before a year was expired," Hall also became critical of the arrangement with the Society. The two printers feuded for another year and then separated, Joseph again buying out his partner.

Through all these vicissitudes, Jeremy carried out his work, poring over the library holdings, selecting items for the separates, and pre-

80. Mass. Hist. Soc., *Procs.*, 1 (1791-1835): 44.

81. A copy of the agreement is in Records of Recording Secretary, 1791-1813, vol. 1.

paring copy for the printers.[82] He also was the key agent in assembling these materials into two more volumes of the *Collections*.

In 1794, Joseph realized he was engaged in a losing venture. He was paying a high price, literally, for familial loyalty. The deteriorating relationship between Joseph and the Society reached a climax in December 1794 when the beleaguered printer appeared before the members and informed them that he could no longer continue the project on the terms of his existing contract. In three years he had lost $400. The project had become a financial liability. If continued, it was certain to lead him into bankruptcy. As he informed the Society: "I found I must necessarily be a looser if I continued the publication at my own risk."[83]

The Society listened politely and then appointed a committee (Belknap was not a member) which was empowered to enter into a contract for the printing business in 1795.[84] In January, the Committee reported that it had signed a contract with Samuel Hall. The Society approved its report.[85]

Joseph was outraged by the Society's action. What particularly galled him was that, under the new arrangement, the Society assumed full financial responsibility for the publication. Hall was to be paid a fee for his service. He assumed no risk whatsoever. Joseph deemed this grossly unfair. He thought he had a "right in all candor to expect the offer of the printing upon the same terms that any other printer would do the work." He appealed for the same consideration as Hall had received. His request was ignored. Thus ended Joseph's relationship with the Society and his career as a Boston printer. The *American Apollo* came to an end on December 24, 1794. Subsequently, Joseph drifted off to the South where he continued to

82. See, for example, a letter from Peter Thacher to Belknap, Feb. 18, 1793, in Records of Corresponding Secretary, 1791-1798.

83. Joseph recounted the history of his firm's relationship with the Society and detailed the financial problems he was experiencing. He appealed for a new and more favorable contractual arrangement. Joseph's written statement on his financial woes is in Records of Recording Secretary, 1791-1813, vol. 1.

84. Mass. Hist. Soc., *Procs.*, 1 (1791-1835): 78.

85. *Ibid.*, 80-81. The Society "threw a bone" to Joseph Belknap by empowering the committee to enter into a contract with him for reprinting 1,000 copies of the "Circular Letter."

flounder in his business ventures. He died in 1800 in Petersburg, Virginia, at the age of 31.[86]

If the schism between the Society and his son's firm was a painful experience for Jeremy, it failed to diminish his interest in either the organization or its publishing program. In July 1795, the Society reevaluated its languishing publishing venture. Failing to formulate a plan or strategy for action, the members appointed Jeremy chairman of a special committee "to investigate and report measures to increase the means of the Society to publish their Collections."[87] Later that year, the Society charged the committee to prepare a statement that was to be printed in the Boston newspapers in an effort to solicit public support.[88]

Belknap prepared the document. After reviewing the history of the publishing program, he appealed to his fellow Bostonians to assist the Society in its effort of "benevolence and public utility." His words transcended the immediate issue and addressed the question of the fundamental purpose of the Society and the responsibility of its members.

Let it be remembered that this Society is formed, not for the purpose of *waiting* for communications, but that the spirit of the Society is *active*; and, besides the Circular Letters, which are sent to every part of the continent and the islands, and which have been reprinted in various periodical publications and in several languages, it is strictly required of every member to search for information of every kind and in every form which may increase the stock of knowledge and enable the Society to be useful.

When it is considered that these Collections will consist of historical and biographical memoirs, geographical and topographical descriptions, accounts of new discoveries and improvements in travels, navigation, manufactures, and commerce, scarce and valuable pamphlets and manuscripts respecting the antiquities of America, and other subjects which daily arrest the attention of the curious and inquisitive, and promise a great increase of science and fund of entertainment, they cannot but hope that a generous and candid public will enable them to carry their views into effect, and assist them in their endeavors to do real service to the community.

86. Mass. Hist. Soc., *Coll.*, 5th ser., 2:484n.

87. Mass. Hist. Soc., *Procs.*, 1 (1791-1835): 86.

88. *Ibid.*, 90.

If the Society were forced to abandon its publications, Belknap warned in his conclusion, "it will be not for want of materials or exertion on their part, but for want of sufficient encouragement on the part of the public; and it will give them extreme pain to record this as one of the characteristics of the American people, that they are backward to encourage the publication of materials for the history of their own country."[89] Like Alexander Hamilton, Belknap did not have strong faith in the "majesty of the masses."

Subsequent events demonstrated that Belknap's lack of faith was justified. His pleading did not result in a surge of financial support for the program. The "generous and candid public" was not responsive. Subscriptions continued to decline. Lacking funds, the Society was forced to suspend publication of the *Collections* in 1796.[90]

But Belknap regarded the program as too important to be allowed to die. In his view, if the public would not support it, the members, corresponding as well as resident, must assume the responsibility. As he informed Corresponding Member Hazard, who had responded to his appeal for support with a gift of $20 in 1797, the resident members had been hard-pressed to sustain the program.

I hope we shall soon make another attempt; and, in that case, we shall solicit help from every part of the continent where we have Corresponding Members. It is in our power to furnish the public with much information, by republishing scarce and valuable pieces, and communicating original matter, which frequently comes into our hands, and would come more frequently, if the publication could be renewed and continued.[91]

Despite Belknap's heroic efforts, the financial problem persisted. Donations from members, resident and corresponding, trickled in slowly. In 1798, the year of Belknap's death, there were sufficient funds on hand to publish volume five of the *Collections*.

While the publication program did not immediately become a rousing success, it was off to a promising start. Again, Belknap was intent upon establishing firm foundations, and he accomplished this objective by his *American Apollo* entries and, more significantly, the

89. The Proposal is printed in *ibid.*, xxx-xxxi.

90. *Ibid.*, 97-98. Nor were the *Collections* published in 1797.

91. Belknap to Hazard, Boston, Aug. 4, 1797, Mass. Hist. Soc., *Coll.*, 5th ser., 3:364.

Collections series. He was personally responsible for the first four volumes. There was no other publication like the *Collections* in the United States. It was a boon to researchers of American history, a seminal source of untold value. In the words of Professor Ebeling, the German scholar: "The Collection of the Historical Society, I say without flattery, is the only source wherein one *may drink deep*, as Pope says."[92]

In addition to publishing historical information, Belknap utilized the *American Apollo* in a number of ways to strengthen the program of the Society. Initially, he used it to assist in the collection of materials. On 15 occasions in the two-year life span of the publication, Belknap inserted articles in which he recorded not only the donations to the Society but also the names of the donors.[93] He knew that people enjoyed seeing their names in print. So long as they were willing to contribute to the program, he was prepared to acknowledge their good works. His usual practice was to preface the list with an expression of warm thanks to the donors, "ladies" as well "gentlemen." On one occasion, he added a reminder of the purposes of the Society and extended an invitation to "gentlemen in all parts of the country to contribute their ingenious and benevolent aid to promote this desireable work. . . . Letters, manuscripts, plans, pamphlets, specimens of natural productions, etc., will be gratefully received and duly acknowledged."[94] Taken *in toto*, the donations listed represent a sizable body of material. He generally listed the gifts by category: for the *Collections*; for the library; for the museum or "cabinet."

The modern bibliophile and librarian, in reviewing Belknap's lists mentioned above, would be quick to notice that the Society acquired many treasured items free of charge. (They also would be envious of such an arrangement.) For example, one can cite such manuscripts as: "fragment of a MS. letter book of Governour [William] Bradford, of Plymouth, from 1624 to 1630, found in a *grocer's shop*, at

92. Ebeling to Belknap, Hamburg, Oct. 1, 1796, Mass. Hist. Soc., *Coll.*, 6th ser., 4:607.

93. *American Apollo*, May 11, June 15, Aug. 3, Aug. 24, and Nov. 30, 1792; Feb. 1, Feb. 8, May 3, Aug. 2, Nov. 1, and Nov. 29, 1793; Jan. 30, Apr. 10, June 19, and July 31, 1794.

94. *Ibid.*, Aug. 24, 1792.

Halifax, N.S."; fragment of the original charter of William and Mary to Massachusetts; and "a large and valuable collection of official papers during the American revolution, made by the late Governour Trumbull of Connecticut." Among printed works, there were such historical headliners as a copy of Cotton Mather's *Magnalia Christi Americana* and the resolves and laws of the Massachusetts colonial legislature. Frequently, because of space limitations, Belknap merely noted the acquisition of "several valuable manuscripts," or "a collection of manuscripts," or "thirty bound volumes, and one hundred pamphlets," or "a number of the first newspapers printed in this country." From the perspective of the 1980s, the historical (as well as financial) value of such materials looms large.

The donations to the museum or "Chamber of Science" were the usual assortment of oddities given to (and collected by) all American historical societies and museums through the early 19th century.[95] For example: "one of the largest kind of Spears used by the Savages on the North West Coast of America"; an "egg of the Ostrich" and some shells from the island of the Indian Ocean; a silver "Denarious" of the Emperor Valentinian "above 1400 years old"; "12 heads" of ancient philosophers, poets, and orators; "One Fly Flap"; "Two Bowling Stones"; a tarantula; a "Golden Cock"; "One Pack of Gambling Sticks"; a "very large Flamingo"; and the jaws and back-bone of a shark.[96]

95. For an informative, as well as humorous, discussion of this subject, see Walter M. Whitehill, ed., *A Cabinet of Curiosities: Five Episodes in the Evolution of American Museums* (Charlottesville, 1967).

96. The Society did not have a formal or well-defined collecting policy and accepted all types of gifts offered to it, even if they bore no relationship to the purpose stated in its act of incorporation. As a result, it acquired many intriguing (and strange) artifacts. Included among these not reported in the *Apollo* were the swords of Miles Standish and William Brewster, "animals preserved in spirits," a Chinese scale and shoe, and a dagger from Malaysia. The donor of the last gift, Thomas H. Perkins, the noted Boston China trader, warned Belknap that Malaysian daggers were frequently poisonous "and I am not certain this is not. I should at least recommend care in shewing it, that the point be avoided." See Perkins to Belknap, Dec. 8, 1794, Records of Corresponding Secretary, 1791-1798.

It would appear that Belknap accepted every gift offered to the Society. In his extant correspondence and official records as corresponding secretary, there is not a single reference to a refusal. It should be noted that, while the Society had an official librarian, Belknap actually received (and deposited) many gifts.

Belknap also inserted notices on scheduled meetings of the Society and the publication of the *Collections*; the latter were directed to the "Friends of History."[97] On one occasion he used a document "taken from the Historical Collections" to provide a detailed description of a theater on Federal Street.[98] The library thus became the source for a "general interest" story.

Belknap also used the paper to publicize the one public lecture the Society sponsored during his lifetime, an address commemorating the third century of Columbus's discovery of America.[99] He had proposed the idea.[100] Held on October 23, 1792, it was a major civic event characterized by ceremonious pomp and unbridled patriotism. After holding their regular quarterly meeting at Peter Thacher's home, the members walked to the Brattle Street Church. Gov. John Hancock, Lt. Gov. Samuel Adams, members of the Council, and other dignitaries were in attendance.

Belknap was the main speaker. The members had "elected" him for the assignment. Prayers and an ode "in concert with the organ" supplemented Belknap's lengthy oration on the great Italian sailor. Following the program, the members of the Society and honored guests assembled at President Sullivan's home for a lavish feast. There "the memory of Columbus was toasted in convivial enjoyment, and the warmest wishes were expressed that the blessings now distinguishing the United States might be extended to every part of the world he had discovered."[101] The Society later published Belknap's "public discourse" and advertised its sale in the *Apollo*.[102]

In persuading the Society to sponsor the Columbus lecture, as well as the *American Apollo* historical segments and the *Collections* se-

---

Until 1794, he held the only key to the Society's quarters. Those wishing to use library materials had to contact him. After 1794, the librarian and cabinet-keeper also were given keys. On the early history of the library, see Samuel A. Green, Mass. Hist. Soc., *Procs.*, 2nd ser., 8 (1892-1894): 312-344.

97. *American Apollo*, Oct. 9, 1794; Mar. 1, 1793; Aug. 21, 1794.

98. *Ibid.*, Nov. 6, 1794.

99. *Ibid.*, Aug. 17, 1792.

100. Mass. Hist. Soc., *Procs.*, 1 (1791-1835): 28-29.

101. *Ibid.*, 45-46; Thomas C. Amory, *Life of James Sullivan*, 2 vols. (Boston, 1859), 1:414.

102. *A Discourse Intended to Commemorate the Discovery of America by Christopher Columbus* (Boston, 1792).

ries, Belknap was affirming that the organization was not exclusively a cloistered gentleman's club. It had a responsibility to promote the common good. By serving as a vehicle for disseminating historical information to the masses, it fulfilled this obligation. Its broader goals were the promotion of "useful knowledge," the creation of a learned, virtuous, and patriotic citizenry, and, at the highest level, the improvement of mankind.

Belknap's vision of the Society as a private organization endowed with a public responsibility to do "good works" was not unusual. In the post-revolutionary period, New Englanders, especially Bostonians, organized scores of private institutions which were designed to serve a multitude of public purposes. These included missionary societies, associations for promoting agriculture, masonic lodges, and a humane society.[103]

Belknap's vision extended to the use of the Society's library, its principal physical resource. He did not regard this facility as the private preserve of members. He held the conviction that any researcher should have access to these materials. He concluded his first "Circular Letter" on November 1, 1791, with this significant statement: "The Library and Museum are deposited in an apartment of Faneuil Hall. ANY PERSON desirous of making a search among the books or manuscripts, may have access to them, under such regulations, as may be known by applying to any one of the members." His emphasis on "any person" is significant. This action underscored his belief in the free use of the Society's historical material.

Belknap was hardly a populist. But he had been heavily influenced by the Enlightenment and was committed to the liberal values of this seminal intellectual movement. Knowledge was for all, not for a select few.

On January 31, 1797, Belknap notified President Sullivan that, because of physical infirmities, he wished to be removed from a spe-

---

103. This development has been analyzed by Richard D. Brown, "The Emergence of Urban Society in Rural Massachusetts 1760-1820," *The Journal of American History*, 61 (1974): 29-51, 37-40; and has been discussed in a doctoral dissertation by Conrad Edick Wright, "Christian Compassion and Corporate Beneficence: The Institutionalization of Charity in New England, 1720-1810" (Brown Univ., 1980).

cial committee appointed in 1795 to prepare a map of the common-wealth, and from all other committees.[104] He continued to attend meetings, however, and collect materials for the library. He also consented to have his name placed in nomination for the position of corresponding secretary, the office he had held from the outset.[105]

Belknap's health rapidly worsened in 1798. He suffered two slight strokes but recovered sufficiently to carry on his ministerial duties and his work in behalf of the Society. To the very end, he was dis-patching letters to prospective donors of materials and gathering historical information. On June 14, for example, he wrote Abigail Adams, requesting information on General John Skey Eustace who had served in the American army during the Revolutionary War. He also inquired whether John Adams "owned Thurloe's State Pa-pers."[106] The wolf was ever on the prowl.

Six days later, on June 20, Belknap suffered an attack of apoplexy which left him paralyzed and speechless. He died later that morning. He was 54 years old. He was buried in the Granary Burying Ground, the resting place of his family and many other Boston worthies, a short distance from his birthplace and beloved historical society.[107]

One month after Belknap's death, the Society held a regular quar-terly meeting at its headquarters, an upper room of Charles Bul-finch's elegant Tontine Crescent.[108] Nineteen members were present. Their first order of business was to elect a new corresponding secre-tary. John Eliot, the librarian, was chosen to replace his close friend. The shifting of Eliot made it necessary to elect a new librarian. John T. Kirkland, the assistant librarian, was tapped for the position. Thomas Wallcut was elected as Kirkland's replacement. The mem-bers directed the recording secretary to buy two volumes of Pur-

104. Belknap to Sullivan, Boston, Jan. 31, 1797, Records of Recording Secre-tary, 1791-1813, vol. 1.

105. Mass. Hist. Soc., *Procs.*, 1 (1791-1835): 105.

106. Belknap to Abigail Adams, Boston, June 14, 1798, Adams Papers, Mas-sachusetts Historical Society. Abigail's response (Philadelphia, June 25, 1798) is printed in Mass. Hist. Soc., *Coll.*, 6th ser., 4: 630-632.

107. On Nov. 22, 1893, the remains of Jeremy and two of his children were moved to the Mt. Auburn Cemetery and buried in a lot owned by his grand-daughter. Information provided by Mt. Auburn Cemetery.

108. This building is illustrated in Mass. Hist. Soc., *Procs.*, 1 (1791-1835), tipped in between 66-67.

chas's *Pilgrims* and the cabinet-keeper to acquire the four-volume edition of Dampier's *Voyages*. They requested President Sullivan to write President Ebenezer Fitch of Williams College and inform him "that the Society will be happy to make such communications and exchanges with the College as will tend to promote the natural, civil, and ecclesiastical history of the country." Functioning in his new capacity, Eliot read a letter from Benjamin Thompson, count Rumford, to the late corresponding secretary in which the noted scientist, statesman, philanthropist, economist, and military leader, now residing in Munich, Germany, graciously acknowledged his election as a corresponding member. While his present "situation and connections" made it difficult for him to cooperate with the Society "in the furtherance of their interesting and useful researches," wrote Rumford, "yet I shall have much pleasure in contemplating, even at this great distance, the fruits of their meritorious exertions; and shall feel no small degree of pride in seeing myself enrolled in the same list with those generous benefactors of future generations whose names will go down to posterity with the treasures they are collecting." The members directed Eliot to have the letter published in one of the Boston newspapers and to mail a set of the Society's *Collections*, "handsomely bound, in four volumes," to the expatriate from Woburn, Massachusetts.

The final item on the agenda dealt with membership. The Society elected two resident members: Benjamin Lincoln and Dr. Isaac Rand; and nominated the Reverend Ebenezer Fitch and John Williams for resident membership, and the Reverend Andrew Eliot of Fairfield, Connecticut, and the Reverend Benjamin Trumbull, of North Haven, Connecticut, for corresponding membership. The latter four would be voted upon at the next quarterly meeting. Adjournment followed.[109]

Though its founder was dead, the Massachusetts Historical Society was very much alive and fit for survival in the years ahead.

109. *Ibid.*, 117-119.

❧ V ❧

Epilogue

He died, alas, too early for your literature and history.

C. D. Ebeling[1]

We have gathered tonight to praise Dr. Belknap and his nine associates, who a century and a half ago set the model for organized historical enterprise in America.

Dixon Ryan Fox[2]

JEREMY BELKNAP'S legacy to American historical scholarship should be considered from two perspectives: his personal contributions as an historian and the significance of the founding of the Massachusetts Historical Society, the "mother society in the country."[3]

As an author of history, Belknap must be judged in the context of his era and his writings weighed against those of his contemporaries. On these bases, he measures up well. He was, as Lawrence Buell has written, "the best regional historian of his day."[4] His *magnum opus*, the *History of New Hampshire*, was an impressive performance for that era, "a milestone in American historiography."[5] Combining scrupulous scholarship and sound literary craftsmanship, it was a solid contribution to American historiography. In Clifford Shipton's words, it "still stands as a priceless record."[6] Almost two centuries after its publication, Belknap's study remains a rich

1. Ebeling to William Bentley, Hamburg, Sept. 16, 1798, "Letters of Christoph Daniel Ebeling," ed. William Coolidge Lane, American Antiquarian Society, *Proceedings*, new ser., 35 (1925): 305-307.

2. "Address at the Celebration of the One Hundred and Fiftieth Anniversary of the Massachusetts Historical Society," Mass. Hist. Soc., *Procs.*, 66 (1936-1941): 411.

3. Edward C. Kirkland's phrase. See *Charles Francis Adams, Jr., 1835-1915, The Patrician at Bay* (Cambridge, Mass., 1965), 207.

4. Lawrence Buell, *New England Literary Culture: From Revolution Through Renaissance* (Cambridge, 1986), 215.

5. Sidney Kaplan, "The History of New Hampshire: Jeremy Belknap as Literary Craftsman," *William and Mary Quarterly*, 3rd ser., 21 (1964): 18.

6. Clifford K. Shipton, *Sibley's Harvard Graduates*, 15:180.

139

and revealing work, still bearing value for students of American history. There is merit in Sidney Kaplan's statement that, had Belknap not died prematurely at the height of his powers, his *History of New Hampshire*, "a pioneer work of American literary-historical art, might well have turned out to be no more than an exercise in preparation for something larger and finer."[7]

Belknap's limited output of historical writings is unfortunate but not surprising. Because of financial necessity, he was forced to work, and, while misplaced in the role of a minister, he was obliged to carry out the full range of duties incumbent upon that office. He thereby lacked sufficient leisure time to ride his "hobby horse" at full speed. He did his historical work piecemeal and at odd hours. His personal letters are suffused with laments at a lack of time to pursue research and writing. "The many duties that are required of me as a son, a husband, a father, a pastor, and a friend, and making allowance for foreseen and unforeseen impediments arising out of the nature of the work," he informed Hazard in 1784, made it likely that he could not produce the second volume of his history of New Hampshire "in less than two, or perhaps three, years from this time."[8]

7. Kaplan, "Jeremy Belknap," 39.

8. Dover, Jan. 13, 1784, Mass. Hist. Soc., *Coll.*, 5th ser., 2:294. When did Belknap find time to pursue his avocation? John T. Kirkland, in his funeral sermon, stated that Belknap was highly disciplined and used his time well. "Not by slighting any of the public or private duties of his office, but by superior economy of time and industry, he redeemed leisure to carry his researches into other fields of literature, suited to gratify his taste and increase his usefulness." See *A Sermon Delivered at the Interment of Jeremy Belknap, D.D. . . .* (Boston, 1798), 12-13. John Eliot offers evidence that Belknap's wife did not favor her husband's practice of spending so much of his spare time poring over historical records and "musty parchments." He wrote Belknap: "You would not do it if you were not above the advice of your wife, in which you shew your good sense, for I heard her scold about when I resided at your house, and know she would have persuaded you off the notion of writing history, to say no more." Eliot to Belknap, Boston, Sept. 18, 1783, Mass. Hist. Soc., *Coll.*, 6th ser., 4:262. Another close friend of the family wrote at the time of Ruth Belknap's death that (after Jeremy's passing) "it was often the occupation of her leisure hours to examine, arrange, and peruse his extensive manuscript collections, and to indulge a fond attention to his favorite objects, by a recurrence to his valuable library." Quoted in Jane B. Marcou, *The Life of Jeremy Belknap, D.D.: The Historian of New Hampshire, with Selections From His Correspondence and Other Writings* (New York, 1847), 245.

Then, too, the lack of an accessible supply of primary sources further limited Belknap's productivity as a scholar. He spent much of his spare time locating and collecting these vital documents. There is much truth in Ebeling's trenchant observation that Belknap lived in the wrong period. He should have lived a generation later.

But this was not his destiny. He was fated to be a pioneer. He blazed a trail for George Bancroft, John L. Motley, John G. Palfrey, Richard Hildreth, Francis Parkman, William H. Prescott, Jared Sparks, and other gentlemen-scholars of Massachusetts who dominated American historical writing in the first decades of the 19th century.[9]

Belknap's enduring contribution to American historical scholarship and to the advancement of humane letters is embodied in the institution he created. By that act, he became the "Founding Father" of the American historical society movement. The establishment of the Massachusetts Historical Society marked the beginning of organized historical research in the United States. For the first time, an institution assumed the responsibility of collecting and preserving reference materials and making them available to researchers and writers of history.

The consequences of Belknap's achievement, this heroic gesture of faith, have been profound. From small beginnings, a powerful movement developed that spread throughout the young nation. The Massachusetts Historical Society became the model for John Pintard's New-York Historical Society (1804), Isaiah Thomas's American Antiquarian Society (1812), and dozens of other societies which sprang up in other states in the early 19th century. All these institutions looked to Belknap's creation as a paragon. Pintard candidly acknowledged the source of obligation in 1805, shortly after founding his "own brat":

Not aspiring to the higher walks of general science, we shall confine the range of our exertions to the humble task of collecting and preserving whatever may be useful to others in the different branches of historical

9. All the eminent historians noted above were members of the Massachusetts Historical Society. Dixon Ryan Fox has written: "Throughout the first eight decades of the nineteenth century most of the distinguished American historians were to be found within the membership of this Society." "Address," 417.

inquiry. We feel encouraged to follow this path by the honourable example of the Massachusetts Historical Society, whose labours will abridge those of the future historian, and furnish a thousand lights to guide him through the dubious track of unrecorded time.[10]

These organizations along the Atlantic seaboard became the base for the vast network of historical societies which has come into being since the mid 19th century and which now extends to every state of the nation. In 1986, the American Association for State and Local History, which serves as the clearinghouse for America's historical societies, estimated that there were 7,000 to 8,000 such organizations in the United States.[11]

These institutions have had a powerful impact upon American educational and cultural life. One can document a strong relationship between these societies and the large quantity of historical research and writing carried out since Belknap's time. The bibliographical references in thousands of historical monographs and articles in professional journals attest to this relationship. It need be emphasized that the societies founded from 1791 to the Civil War acquired the bulk of the most significant source materials pertaining to the early history of the United States. A number of these institutions now rank among the leading research repositories in the nation—for example, the Massachusetts Historical Society, the New-York Historical Society, the American Antiquarian Society, the Historical Society of Pennsylvania, and the Virginia Historical Society.

Until well into the 19th century, only historical societies collected source materials. As the nation's cultural and educational systems expanded and matured, and as a growing legion of historians appeared, other types of institutions, both public and private, were founded and became involved in this activity. The Library of Congress, the National Archives and presidential libraries, state and municipal archival programs, college and university libraries, independent research libraries—the list of institutions now serving the needs of historians, amateur and professional, numbers in the thou-

10. "Address to the Public, The New-York Historical Society," *New York Herald*, Feb. 13, 1805.

11. Letter to the author from Gerald George, then director of American Association for State and Local History, Feb. 28, 1986.

sands. No other nation in the world can match this variegated network of research repositories. As a consequence, the modern historian is blessed with a cornucopia of sources. As Harvard University Librarian Paul Buck impishly noted in 1961, "catering to his [the historian's] needs (real or fancied) is like throwing peanuts to pigeons, or shoveling corn to swine." And Buck added this solemn reminder: "There was a time when the historian had to collect his own material."[12]

In studies which examine the cultural and intellectual history of the United States, Belknap rarely receives more than a fleeting reference. He deserves greater recognition. He was a cultural pioneer of the first rank, one of Clio's most faithful consorts. He founded an institution and inspired many others which, collectively, furnish a thousand lights to guide historians through "the dubious track of unrecorded time."

12. *The Historian, the Librarian and the Businessman*, address at dedication of Eleutherian-Mills Historical Library (Wilmington, 1961).

Index